To Market, To Market,

To Market, To Market,

The Story of Ashton-under-Lyne's Ancient Market

Philip Martin Williams
& David L. Williams

History on your Doorstep

Published in Great Britain
by History on Your Doorstep
(HOYD Publishing)
15 Welbeck House
Welbeck Street South
Ashton-under-Lyne
Lancs. OL6 7TB
Tel: 0161 308 3013
Email: hoyd@btinternet.com

First Published 1994.
Reprinted 1995, 1998.

New Edition 2009

ISBN 978-09518012-6-0

Dedication

This book is dedicated to the memory of both our Mother & Grandmother, whose visits together to Ashton Market were part of a regular Saturday tradition

Acknowledgements

We would like to acknowledge the many people who aided in the creation of the original book and also this revised edition.

We begin by offering our sincere gratitude to Ryan M. Williams, who first conceived the idea of a history of Ashton Market, whilst still at school for his chosen project. His completed work gave us the inspiration and a strong basis from which to start.

Many thanks to Alice Lock and the staff at The Tameside Local Studies Library, for use of their extensive newspaper files and also for providing numerous books and documents. A special thank you to John Hodgson of the John Rylands Institute, Manchester who made available for our perusal a number of ancient documents and also happily translated the original Ashton market charter. We are also indebted to past market managers Mr Lorenzo O'Reilly and Philip Poulter along with the present Markets Business Development Manager Mr H. Ian Kelly,

In addition we also acknowledge the following for use of their photographs and illustrations, Tameside Local Studies Library, Tameside Reporter, The National Trust (Stamford Archive - John Rylands Library, Manchester), Elsie Houlton, Marks & Spencer PLC, Philip Poulter, John Walters, David Conn, Ken Rogerson, Leonard Corns, Mrs E Finnerty, Rita Hunter, Derek Duckworth, Roy Taylor with special thanks to Howard Murphy Tameside MBC and The Tameside Advertiser.

We are also obliged to the many market traders past and present and to members of the public who allowed themselves to be interviewed for the purpose of this book, including, Leonard Corns, Alfred Entwistle, Professor Harold Gilbert, John Latus, Harvey Wright, Fred and Barbra Rust, Kim Wright, Barry Gleave, Harriet Clegg, Rita Hunter, Derek Duckworth, Alan and Ruth Rhodes, Roy Taylor, Jason Beeley, Sid Williams, Sheila Hooton and to the others, to numerous to mention who contacted us with their many interesting stories and anecdotes.

We apologise in advance for any unintentional omissions and would be pleased to insert the appropriate acknowledgement in any subsequent editions of the book. Finally, a thank you to Sharon Taylor for her drawing on page 10 and a special thanks to Bill Tarmey for kindly writing the foreword.

The rhymes used as chapter headings (1-6) in the book are from: 'The Nursery Rhymes of England', as collected by James Orchard Halliwell and first published in 1842.

Foreword.

By Bill Tarmey

I was once asked why I had never moved out to live in some Cheshire village like many other television and sporting personalities. My reply was why should I? I was born in Ardwick, Manchester, moving to the Bradford area of the city when just a few months old. I grew up in a small two up two down terraced house which leaned somewhat sideways and if you weren't in bed by nine o'clock the bugs would come and get you.

As a kid I worked on Grey Mare Lane Market for a number of traders including a jeweller and greengrocers. Then I began working for a guy called John Seldon – whom courtesy of my good friends Philip and David Williams can be found in the pages of this wonderful book. John worked four or five markets at that time but my favourite was always Ashton Market – which we would visit every day. Around seven-thirty each morning we would provide lamps for stallholders at Grey Mare Lane before climbing into John's 'big van' for the short journey to Ashton. I always called it the 'big van' but it was more like a converted bus with the seats taken out.

On arrival at Ashton, once again we would hire out the lamps to various traders – these lamps were not just for light but were also useful for keeping the traders warm especially on those bitterly cold mornings. After that task had been completed came the hard job of erecting the roundabout – or juvenile as we called it – which unlike the ones on the market today had to be erected and dismantled daily. Many a time on a Saturday John would leave me to operate the roundabout when he went off for a drink with his brother. I would turn the handle so the kids could have their ride and I was not much older than they were. All in all it was really hard work – but I loved it. I was paid three bob a day (three shillings). A halfcrown and a sixpence piece. I'd go home and put the money down on the table, 'there you are mum'. She would say 'the tanner's yours'. So, a sixpence then for my efforts, life was tough but I was helping. Life on the market was tough but it was also great. I really enjoyed the market whether I was working or just strolling around the stalls.

I still love markets and market towns today and Ashton is one of the best and that's one reason why I've not joined the Cheshire Country set. The memories come flooding back each time I accompany my grandchildren to the roundabouts and I too was shocked and saddened the day fire destroyed the market hall - All that history and peoples' livelihoods gone up in smoke. Philip and David have thankfully brought this book right up to date so that once again we can all reminisce as the story of Ashton's Ancient Market leaps from every page. I hope you enjoy reading 'To Market, To Market' as much as I did.

Lets all look ahead with hope that the new market hall will have the same impact upon Ashton as its predecessor and that the town will always remain a great town.

Bill Tarmey
Ashton-under-Lyne 2009

Bill Tarmey with authors Philip (left) and David Williams

Preface.

Part of the stained glass window which prior to the fire of 2004 could be seen above the centre Bow Street market entrance

The origins of Ashton-under-Lyne Market obviously begin with the granting to the town of a Royal Charter. However, the point at which Ashton first received this grant has been a contentious issue for many years. There are those, ourselves included, who believe that this was in 1413, others however would make claim to an earlier date of 1284.

One can understand why Tameside Council believe the early date to be true after all it does almost add a further 130 years of heritage when promoting the market and town. The council's official web-site proudly proclaims 1284 as too do other popular non-official town web-sites, sites which thousands of people log on to for information regarding Ashton. The fact remains though, that there has never been any trace of a document or evidence to indicate that a 1284 charter ever existed. The only so-called 'proof' came from Edwin Butterworth in his book *'History of Ashton-under-Lyne'* (1842) when he stated that he had seen a document attributing the charter as being granted by King Edward I in 1284. He even fails to state what this document was. During the course of time other writers used Butterworth's claim as being 'fact', Mrs Bowman in her book *'England in Ashton-under-Lyne* (1960) repeated the assertion again citing his work as 'proof'.

With reference to a charter being granted in 1413 this cannot now be doubted or questioned. Several years ago the actual charter was discovered amongst papers of the Stamford Estate at Dunham Massey. The wording on this charter signed by King Henry IV clearly states the granting of a market from 1413 – see chapter one. Having seen this ancient document we must certainly agree with Michael Nevell's statement in his book *'Tameside 1066-1700', (1991)* "...the lack of any mention of an earlier market in the 1413 grant makes... [Butterworth's claim] ...highly unlikely, and this [1284] document must be treated as spurious". Michael Nevell's book was one of a series commissioned by Tameside Council so it seems strange that they don't stand by his beliefs. The 1413 date was also accepted by Tameside's former local history librarian, Mr C. Wilkins-Jones *('Tameside, An Outline History', 1978)* and by G.H. Tupling *('An Alphabetical List of Markets and Fairs of Lancashire Recorded Before the Year 1701', 1936)*. In 1993, the highly respected Head of Local Studies, Alice Locke said; "It does seem very unlikely that two market charters would have been granted".

Throughout the extensive research for this book, we have failed to unearth a single shred of evidence to support Butterworth's statement. Today it seems that most people with the exception of Tameside Council acknowledge the 1413 charter as being *'the charter'* and accordingly it is to the Ashton-under-Lyne of the 15th century that we turn to start our story.

Chapter One.

To market, to market to buy a fat pig,
Home again, home again jiggedy jig;
To market, to market to buy a fat hog,
Home again, home again joggedy jog.

Ashton Town with Market Cross and Market House (right) as it would have looked sometime after 1800

Ashton-under-Lyne during the 15th century was a rural community covering the areas of Ashton Town, Audenshaw, Hartshead and Knott Lanes, and was reliant on mixed farming for its livelihood. Initially, the growing of cereal crops like oats were the main produce, but later, the keeping and rearing of livestock became more increased. The embryo of today's town centre Ashton grew from a small settlement near to the church of St. Michael's, on the west bank of the River Tame, which soon became the hub of the local farming community. The local population was capable of producing enough food for its own use, and there may well have been times when surplus amounts were grown which could then be sold. Selling it however, prior to the setting up of Ashton's own market, would have resulted in the need to make the taxing and hazardous journey to market at Manchester. Travelling along the difficult uneven cart tracks that passed for roads, through the swampy, marshy areas of Ashton Moss and on through Littlemoss and Failsworth. Therefore, the granting of a royal charter to Sir John de Assheton by King Henry IV on February 13th,

1413, enabling Ashton to hold its own market, would have undoubtedly been welcomed by all in the manor. Although originally written in Latin, the following full translation conveys the sense of the document sufficiently clearly; *Henry, by the grace of God, King of England and France and Lord*

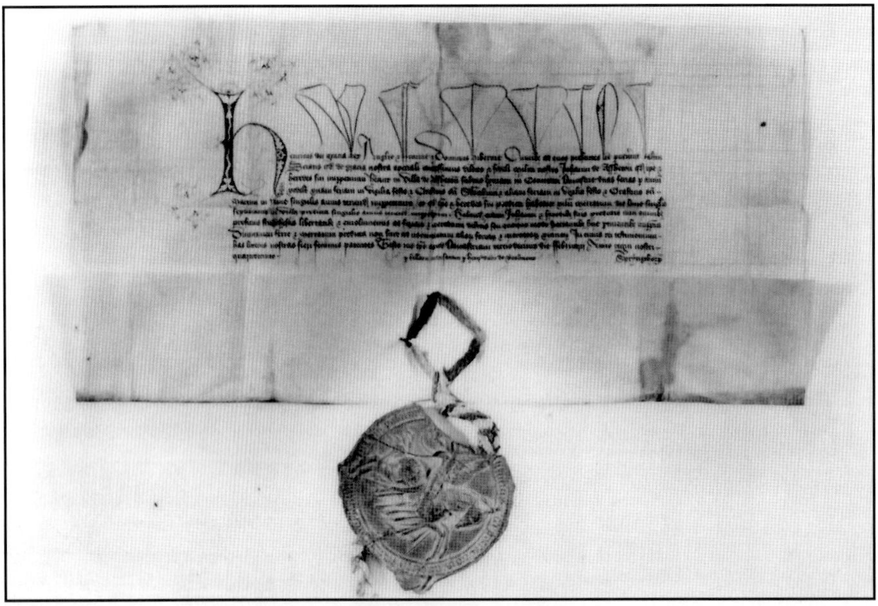

The original Ashton-under-Lyne Market Charter – found in recent years among papers at Dunham Massey.

of Ireland, to all whom the present letters shall come, Greetings. Know that by our special grace we have granted to our beloved and faithful knight John de Assheton that he and his heirs for ever may have in the town of Ashton-under-Lyne in the county of Lancaster two fairs annually, namely one fair on the eve, the feast day and the morrow of St. Swithen's, and the other fair on the eve, the feast day and the morrow of St. Martin in the Winter, to be held in the said town forever, and that he and his said heirs may hold one market on Monday each week in the said town forever. To hold to the same John and his heirs with all profits, franchises, liberties and emoluments due to or in any way relating or pertaining to a fair and market for ever, provided that the said fairs and market do not harm other neighbouring fairs and markets. In witness whereof we have caused these our letters to be made patent. Witnessed by myself at Lancaster the thirteenth day of February in the fourteenth year of our reign. Thirty-five days after putting his name to the document King Henry IV died.

The two fairs granted were not, of course, to be of the kind we know and enjoy today, but were welcomed annual events where merchants from far and wide would come with all manner of foreign and exotic items. Goods and cattle were also bought and sold and local farmers may have also used them for the purpose of recruiting farm labour. Although not the pleasure fairs of today, there would nonetheless still have been an abundance of entertainment to be enjoyed with jugglers, dancers, bear-baiting and dog-fighting. These two fairs would continue as part of Ashton's community life for over 400 years.

At the period when Ashton first established its market, the town would have been no more than just a few small dark streets. These being Towne Street (later Scotland Street) which ran north from the manor house or 'old hall' as it was known, past St. Michael's church and on up to a village green, from where it joined Old Street, which ran in a westerly direction, out of town, towards Manchester. The village green was the spot where the original market cross was erected and where of course, the markets were held. In keeping with the period, Ashton's first market cross was probably no more than a simple structure, though perhaps local tradesmen could have been responsible for making something more elaborate. The cross would, over the oncoming centuries, have been replaced on many occasions, and may have altered in its appearance. Whatever changes in style to the cross may have occurred, its position remained fairly static, always being in the locality of what today is referred to as St. Michael's Square.

According to the custom and rental roll of 1422, there were, in addition to the church and 'old hall', about 30 buildings, two-thirds of which would have been small cottages, whilst the others would have been made up of craftsmen's workshops, like the village smithy. Another important building was the tollbooth which was erected near to the market area. It was here that all tolls and charges in respect of the market would have been paid, before finding their way into the coffers of the lord of the manor. When, in July 1515, Sir Thomas, the last Lord de Assheton died, it was stated in his will that the manor of Ashton was to be divided between his daughters, Elizabeth Assheton and Alice Hoghton, and his grandson, George Booth, son of another daughter, Margaret. According to W. Bowman in her book 'England in Ashton-under-Lyne', Ashton's market may have ceased to operate for a time after Thomas de Assheton's death. A possible reason for this, she says, is that there could have been problems created by the division of the manorial tenure between joint heirs. If the market had indeed ceased at that time, then it must certainly have recommenced by 1608; For at this time, with the 1413 charter thought lost, a namesake and descendant of the aforementioned George Booth applied for and received confirmation of the market rights.

With the market rights being reaffirmed it is difficult to understand why there may have been another short period of discontinuance, for in 1628, local clergyman Rector Fairfax, wrote of Ashton... *"this being no market town".* However, there is also a claim to say that there was a market operating in Ashton just five years later. For in the John Rylands Library in Manchester, there is a document attesting to the ancientness of the market, made under oath in 1703. One statement made by John Newton says that he had known it to be a market town for 70 years and upwards. Taking the date of the document into account, it is clear that John Newton could recall a market in Ashton in 1633 and even quite possibly earlier.

When the old toll booth was replaced by a new purpose built Market House in 1636 it is quite possible that a new Market Cross was also erected to coincide with this. There is certainly evidence to show that a new cross was erected in 1763/4 and one with which care was taken in its construction. The total costs involved in the production of this cross amounted to £5. 4s. 1d. with £2. 15s. of this being paid to Joseph Hampson as the main craftsman involved. This particular cross consisted of a solid oak structure standing upon a stone base topped by a painted sphere or crown. Yet, as impressive a structure as this cross may have been for some unknown reason it too was replaced by another some thirty-five years later (1798).

Since its opening, the Market House had become the centre of operations for the 'Market Lookers' and traders alike. It was here where the payments and tolls were made and where petty disagreements and squabbles were settled. The 'Market Lookers' were a type of early market inspectors who also acted as weights and measure officers and checked on traders to see that their wares were suitable and fit for sale. At this time Ashton had its own official weights and measures and these were used to test the individual weights used by traders. All weights corresponding with 'Town Weights' as they were known, were affixed with an official seal, while any that showed inaccuracies resulted in the trader being fined. It is recorded that one William Walker, a market looker in 1783, during the course of his duty, summoned trader Thomas Mayal... *"for having 3 false and unsealed weights and for much insulting him in the execution of his office".* Josia Booth, a trader in 1789, was fined for... *"selling 2 pounds of salt 4 ounces short of 'weight of the town'."* On each market day before any trading could commence, the town crier or 'Bellman' as he was known in Ashton, had first to clearly ring his bell. Any transaction that took place before this opening procedure would again result in the trader being fined. Any trader being caught breaking rules or being fined on more than four occasions was held to public ridicule when confined to a period in the local stocks.

In 1795 another claim that the town's market had fallen into disuse was made by J. Aikin in his book 'A Description of the Country Thirty to Forty Miles round Manchester'. Aikin stated... *"there was formerly a market held here every Wednesday, at a place where an ancient cross is still standing; it has been discontinued above thirty years,* [since 1762] *though such a convenience is now particularly wanted, from the rapidly increased population".* This claim was also later repeated in a publication by Edward Baines. It seems that this claim can be dismissed, as W. Bowman confirms in her book, when she states... *"toll of the market* [in 1794] *still took its annual place amongst the manorial receipts, so it is difficult to understand Aikin's statement of 1795, which is obviously incorrect".* Aikin seems to have been correct when he stated that markets had been held on Wednesdays, for although the main market day was always Monday, a number of the statements in the aforementioned 1703 document attest to a Wednesday market. Perhaps, as Aikin was not a local man, he was unaware of the Monday main market day, and if any market day had ceased, perhaps it had just been the minor Wednesday market.

The cross referred to by Aikin in 1795 must have been the one which was erected in 1763/4. Yet in 1798, just three years after his reference this cross was also replaced. It is however, uncertain whether the whole of the extant structure was renewed or if it was simply the top part – the oak shaft which was altered. It is possible that the cross's original base and steps remained while a new stone top piece was erected bearing the inscription 'Erected by Thos Walker, Japh Knight, Robert Lees, Thos [Evans?] 1798. What is certain is that the whole structure was moved to a slightly different location now being positioned in the roadway adjacent to the Market House at the foot of Old Cross Street.

Since the 16th century Ashton had developed a thriving textile cottage industry and therefore found itself more able to adapt to the industrial revolution of the late 1700's and early 1800's. With the invention of the steam engine, purpose built cotton mills were erected in the town, and the work generated by these attracted more and more people into the area from outlying regions and beyond. As a direct result of the growth in work, the population of Ashton Parish in 1801 had increased to 15,632, a rise of 10,535 on the population count of 1775, and the biggest effect of this boom in population was felt in the old centre of Ashton near to the church and market house. There was now a great deal more traffic passing through the town as in recent years more roads had been laid. The main street to Manchester was now New Street (later Stamford Street) and crossing this at various points were many other smaller roads.

All this was having its effect on the market and certainly by 1820 the old market site was obviously inadequate. The traders which were still coming in to town were desperate to sell their wares where best they could – so much so that they were prepared to contravene local laws by setting up their stalls along nearby streets. Continuously the Court Leet were warning people and imposing fines on those whose stalls were causing inconvenience to pedestrians and hindering the flow of traffic. One trader fined in 1822 for doing this was James Fletcher who had to pay the penalty for erecting his stall on the footpath of George Street. With the population now standing at 25,967 the worsening conditions could hardly be allowed to continue and it was generally thought that if the town wanted a market then a new site desperately needed to be found and one that would also allow for future expansion. With this in mind, in 1823 the Earl of Stamford and Warrington promised a plot of land comprising 14,000 sq yards for use as a market – though it would be quite some time before any plans were implemented.

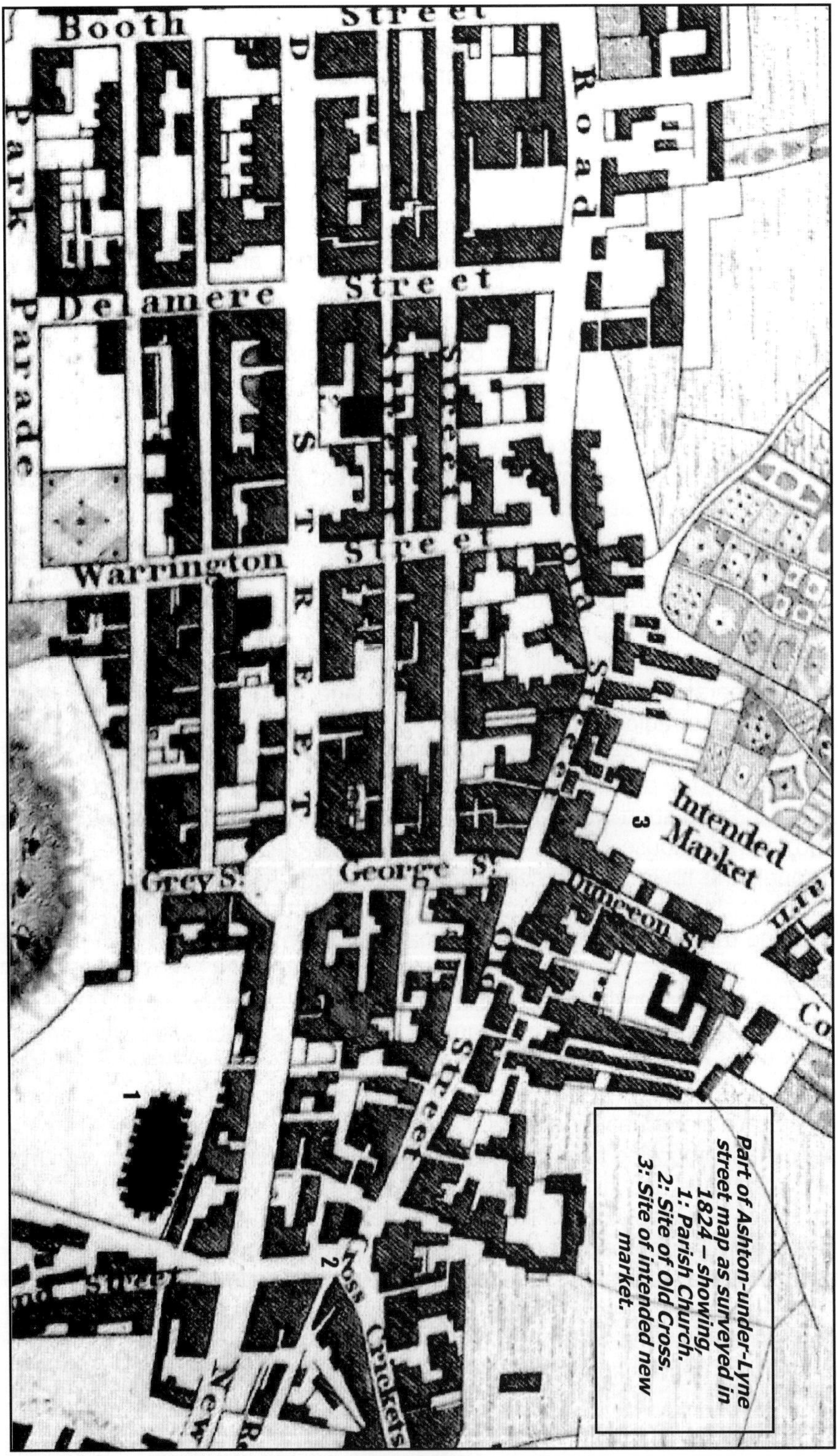

Part of Ashton-under-Lyne street map as surveyed in 1824 – showing, 1: Parish Church. 2: Site of Old Cross. 3: Site of intended new market.

Ashton's staggering population increase had for some time been making the Court Leet's task of administrating the town an almost impossible one. However, it was to be another four years before moves to rectify this situation came about with the introduction in 1827 of what was termed 'The Police Act'. This 'Act' gave over the running of the town to Commisioners – made up of rate-payers and the powers for them to oversee everything from Street Lighting to Cleansing and all Town Improvements.

In December 1827 a public meeting was held to obtain the consent of the commissioners for an application to be made to Parliament to amend 'The Police Act' and obtain power to regulate the market and erect a market place in Ashton. Mr John Whitehead chaired the meeting in which a Mr Lord spoke at length about the advantages which would arise from having a market. Mr Swire and Mr Harrop both fully agreed to the proposed market with the latter reminding all present that the Earl of Stamford's sole wish was to benefit the town with a market. Other commissioners attending were Mr Southern and Mr Algar and by the conclusion of the meeting several resolutions had been put forward and approved.

With the wheels of power turning slowly in respect of the new market the traders which remained were continuing to sell their goods from any point they could and by 1828 what amounted to a permanent Saturday evening street market had developed and proved highly popular.

The prospect of a new market took another step forward when the ownership of the land designated for this purpose was officially transferred on June 5th 1829 with the official document proclaiming, *"I the Earl of Stamford being well satisfied that the providing of a market place would be to the advantage of the town and public in general, freely and voluntarily give the plot of land unto the said commissioners for such a market place, without receiving any consideration for same."* The document went on to say that the land should be... *"for the only purpose of being used as a market for the town".* Although the land had been freely given, the Earl did receive some sort of payment, with the sum of £20 being paid annually, which was probably in compensation for the loss of rents on a number of dwellings occupying the land which were consequently demolished. This piece of land described as lying between Old Street and Style Barn was 14,000 yds in total with 12,053 yds being used for the market and open market ground with the rest being taken up by the new access road eventually to become Bow Street. There was much work to be done with the land before any market could materialise – including the removal of Dungeon Street, once part of Cow Hill Lane which was to be replaced by a much wider Market Street. The very first stalls to be built were erected in brick and ran down three sides of a flagged area with an open side fronting the new Market Street. With the initial traders all being local butchers – soon to be joined by a number of centrally placed fish stands – the enclosure became known as 'The Shambles' this being an ancient term for a meat market or area where butchery took place. This then was to be the beginning of what eventually would become the Market Hall, these early stalls in relation to the hall (before the fire of 2004), would have formed the central portion and it is quite possible that 'The Off Licence', 'Budget Jewellery' and 'Williams' Café' were actually three of the original butchers stalls.

Possibly 'Williams' Café' 'Budget Jewellery' and 'The Off Licence' were three of the original butchers stalls.

Whilst work was still ongoing a number of stalls opened for trading in July 1829 almost twelve months before the official opening of the market on July 2nd 1830. The principal market day was now to be Saturday with other markets also held on Mondays and Wednesdays. On completion at a cost of £4,000 there was a total of twentysix stalls with rents raging from £10 to £13 per year.

With the opening of the new market ground, the Market House at the old site took on a new purpose and the market cross was taken down. There is evidence to show that in 1821-3 the cross was still an imposing feature standing as it did on its raised base. However, by 1827 it was being described as *"a small cross"* which indicates that for some reason it had once again been modified with now only the top two sections surviving. After its final removal the remaining part of the cross was put in the hands of Isaac Watt Boulton, an eminent local engineer who for some considerable time kept it safe before it eventually found its last resting place within Stamford Park. Incidentally, the cross that today stands within the St. Michael's Square area is a replica of this last cross. The old Market House soon became known as the 'Court House' and was used by the local Magistrate well into the 1880s – the building was finally demolished in 1889. The 'Court House' also continued to be used by the commissioners up to 1840 as a base for administrating the town. At this point a new 'Town Hall' was erected at a cost of £7,500 (with its size being virtually trebled in 1879 at a further cost of £16,000).

Gradually since its opening in 1830 the new market place had become quite an attraction with traders and townsfolk alike – not an attractive place but certainly a busy one. By the 1840's the number of traders setting

(Above Left): ***Ashton Market Cross from street plan surveyed in 1824.***

(Above Right): ***The remains of the old Ashton Market Cross as it stands today in Stamford Park.***

(Below): ***The Market House – awaiting demolition in 1889.***

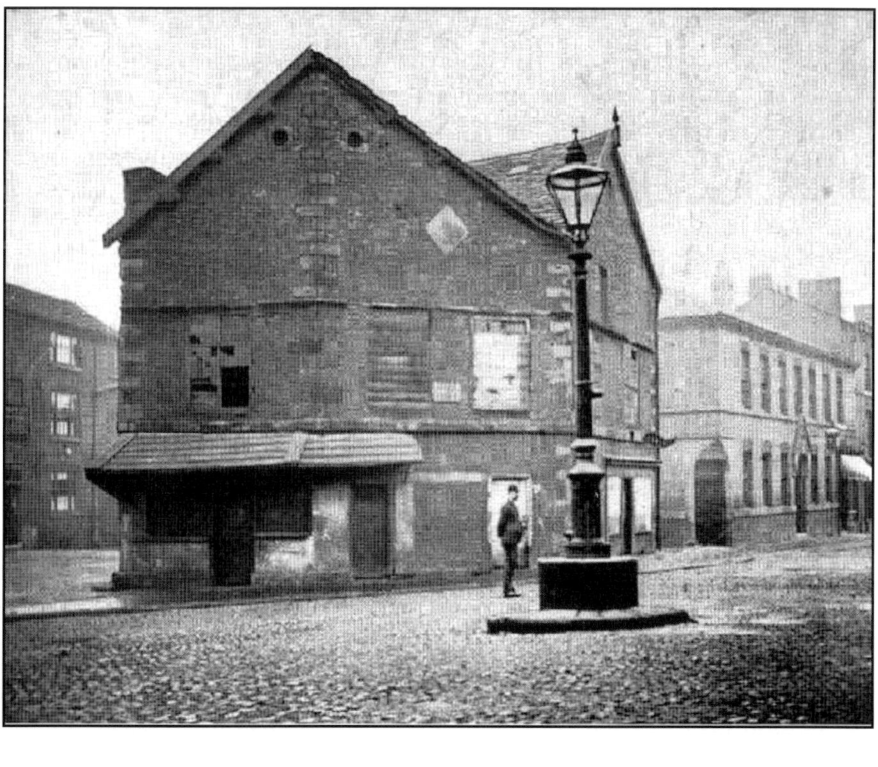

An artist impression of the Bow Street side of the market in 1830 based on photographs taken of the original wall revealed after the fire of 2004.

up stalls on the market ground had increased and on market days the whole area was a busy and noisy environment. The butchers and especially the fisherwomen in the Shambles would each attempt to outdo one another as they shouted out their wares. During April 1843 two such fisherwomen, Margaret Butler and Mary Goodwin, had for a number of weeks caused some concern with their bellowing. This had now become more of a personal feud as the pair continued to shout abuse and obscenities towards each other. Mary Goodwin appeared to have been the winner as Margaret Butler seemed unable to match her vocal prowess – so much so that Margaret decided to take her rival to court in the hope that they would silence her. Margaret went armed with a witness who unfortunately, when called said that both parties were as bad as each other. The court dismissed them both basically with no more than a flea in their ears. However, the same Mary Goodwin found herself once again in front of the Magistrate just two months later – on this occasion she had been summoned by Constable Maiden for selling unwholesome fish. Mrs Goodwin had the court house in fits of laughter when in her defence she explained that she didn't sell fish but sold prawns and shrimps and produced from her pocket a handful of the same, thrusting them upward to the Magistrate as if to prove her point. After receiving a lesson as to the term 'fish' she was fined 2s 6d with

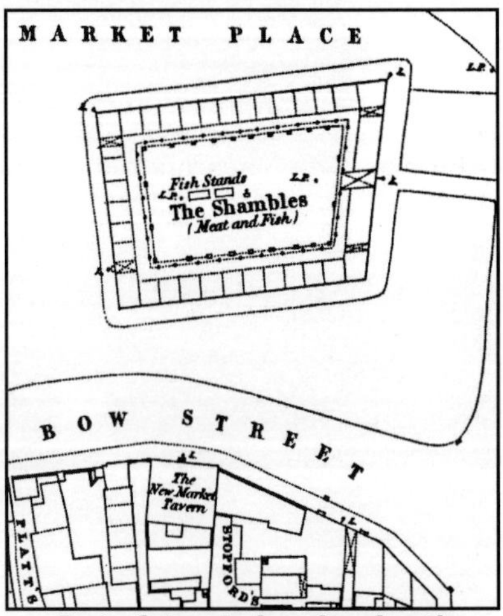

Part of street plan showing the market and the central meat and fish 'Shambles'.

costs. Each day the town constables as part of their duty would make sure everything at the market was being run in the approved manner. During the first few weeks of 1844 Constable Maiden and his colleague had reason to warn several butchers for selling beef which was unfit for sale. These butchers, who usually sold poorer quality meat than the others, had joined together to purchase the beef, which was divided between them and mixed with the good meat they had on display. Despite the warnings butcher James Kenyon was summoned before the magistrate for selling decayed beef. He was duly fined 12s with six weeks hard-labour should he default. Seven days later Henry Lees Ogden, a butcher in the Shambles was also before the court on a similar charge. Again Constable Maiden and his colleague Constable Key gave evidence as too did the meat inspectors Cuttle and Slater who told the court that the meat was from a cow that had died of disease. The Magistrate, Mr Lord fined Mr Ogden £1 plus costs and also warned him that should he be brought before him again the highest penalty allowed by law would be enforced. For a number of weeks around this time it seems that the practice of selling bad meat had increased and was beginning to worry the authorities, however the court was now vowing to play its part in the suppression of this objectionable act and to protect the public.

In 1835 the Municipal Corporation Act, sometimes known as the Municipal Reform Act came into being. This Act of Parliament introduced what would become modern local government, for it required members of town councils (municipal corporations) in England and Wales to be elected by rate-payers. Borough Councils elected in this way were empowered to take on responsibility for policing, public health and education and were subject to regulation and auditing which served to reduce corruption. Many industrial towns of the north and midlands, including Manchester quickly acted by petitioning for incorporation, which was achieved by the city in 1838. In Ashton-under-Lyne a public meeting was held on February 18th 1847 from which a petition for a charter of incorporation was sent to the Queen, this was duly granted on September 29th 1847. From this time onward the powers and provisions of the Municipal Corporation Act were extended to Ashton and on November 22nd the first election of councillors took place.

On February 7th 1848, the newly-formed council received from the former commissioners of the town, the deeds transferring ownership to them of the market and market ground. The council sought help from parliament in their quest to advance the town, and received it with the passing of the town improvement act in 1849. This now gave them the ability to borrow up to £20,000 to spend on improvements, including the power to extend and erect market places and also to increase local rates in order to pay for same.

Ashton's famous 'Market Avenue' probably the town's first ever pedestrianised shopping thoroughfare was born out of this time. Joseph Fletcher was the inspiration and financial backer behind transforming what was once, according to the Reporter, "*...tumbledown filthy dwellings and fever dens, the resort of thieves, prostitutes and beggars".* Joseph Fletcher had started in business as an Old Street corn dealer before acquiring a number of other business interests and becoming owner of several mills, including 'Birch Mills'. He was responsible for ridding the town of many run-down properties, buying them up for redevelopment; Fletcher Street, off Market Street, bears his name. The plans for the market avenue were drawn up by the established firm of John Eaton and Sons, and according to a plaque at the Stamford Street entrance, work began in 1847, while another plaque at the Old Street junction would indicate it was completed in 1849. For quite some time after being opened, the market avenue was known as 'Fletcher's Arcade'. As it does to this day, the avenue contained many shops and services and helped in securing Ashton's reputation as a growing shopping centre.

Plaque at the Stamford Street entrance to the Market Avenue.

If asked to picture mentally a butcher from this period, most people would probably come up with an archetypal large pot-bellied, jolly chap, probably with striped apron and straw boater, which in fact, wouldn't be too far removed from the truth. One writer contributing to the local paper in 1900, looked back to the market of 1850 and recalled: "*when you entered the market hall, the butchers in stentorian tones shouted the quality of their meat, and to get past these flesh dealers rubicund visages and full-bodied rotundity was a task".* It must have also been quite a task to walk on the outside market place, for the ground was just dirt and would have suffered very badly during any adverse weather conditions. Whatever the climate might have been, it would certainly not have stopped the many traders from gathering there, and quite a noise they made too as each tried to out-shout one another in proclaiming their wares. Horns, drums and all manner of musical instruments were used to attract customers and not to be outdone; the hardware dealer would clash his pots and pans. If the shoppers seemed to be ignoring the crockery stall, then their attention would soon be drawn back to it as the seller would occasionally 'accidentally' smash pots. This mishap no doubt drew crowds to which the trader would instantly switch his sales patter. Greengrocers and fruit merchants vied with each other for the lion's share of the trade with each loudly implying that their goods alone were of the highest quality. "*The fruiterers generally sold eggs and sometimes these would be 28 for 1s*". One of the most popular stalls upon the market at this time was the hot pea or pea-soup stall, which no doubt did good business during the winter months when for a halfpenny the shopper could choose between black or green peas.

Over the last 30 years the town's population had expanded two-fold to reach an incredible 56,959 and for many of these people a trip to the market was just like popping out to the corner shop; for the immediate vicinity of the market now consisted of a densely populated area, with streets like Gosforth Street, Jermyn Street, Tatton Street, Katherine Street, Delamere Street, Cotton Street, and Duke Street all containing rows of small terraced houses.

With their newly acquired powers under the 'improvement act' council meetings held during the early part of 1851 included many discussions regarding the enlargement of the market. On August 13th it was proposed that the sum of £1,700 be borrowed to expand the existing market building, but just ten days later at the next meeting plans that had been submitted by architects and reviewed by the market committee were rejected. It was decided instead that the committee should advertise for two new sets of plans, (one each for the south (Bow Street) and east (Market Street) sides of the market) for the purpose of... "*erecting a market covering upon iron pillars with glass and slate roof*". Plans and agreements must have finally been reached that were to the satisfaction of the market committee, for by August of 1852 the extension had been built, and the committee was now urging that the project should have the finishing touches put to it by the erecting of necessary stalls and other conveniences. One of the first tenants to work inside the market extension was William Bailey who originally began trading with children's toys from one of the new stalls. Later after changing over to hardware he expanded his business with further stalls. Up until the early 1990s two stalls were still trading, one hardware the other electrical, and although these were no longer associated with the same family they both still proudly retained the 'Bailey' name for all to see. However, in November 1993 the hardware stall closed for business to be taken over by MG Carpets.

A rare glimpse of the original outer wall with boarded up window in 1993.

Several alterations were required to convert the hardware stall into one suitable for carpet sales and it was during this conversion work that an opportunity arose to catch a rare sight of the original outside wall of the building. Clearly visible were several boarded-up window frames complete with protruding windowsills. Taking in this sight, along with that of the adjacent archway it wouldn't have been difficult to visualise the building's appearance as it had once been, prior to the erection of the 1852 extension. Also near to the Bailey's Electrical stall could be seen one of the iron pillars that helped to support the roof of the extension, this like many of the others around the hall carried the inscription 'Thacker & Son AD 1852'.

Although there is no record to show when the new market extension actually opened to the public, it would almost certainly have been sometime after the aforementioned August meeting and prior to December 1st when new market bye-laws came into force. While the 1852 extension was as suggested 'a roof supported by iron pillars' it appears that it was only the south side which was actually walled. This is born out by the Market & Lighting Committee meeting in August 1856 when they were advocating the walling on the east side. It was stated that..."*The east side of the market was open, and the consequence was that the stands on that side had scarcely ever been let. If the market was walled round, it could be locked up; and then the butchers might leave their claps open in summer, and their meat would not spoil".* It is not known when this issue was finally dealt with but it is quite possible that work was not actually carried out until the next extension was built in 1867.

With the opening of the 1852 extension and the introduction of new bye-laws Ashton's shopping area not only took on a different look but also developed a whole new atmosphere. The main contributing factor to this being, that now traders were no longer allowed to make any loud sounds whatsoever in trying to draw the shoppers' attention to their stalls. As a result, compared to previous years, shopping was now carried out in comparative silence, no more could be heard the bellowing of the traders voices or blasts from instruments. This of course is not to say that traders were averse to breaking the rules, for no doubt many tried, not always successfully, however, as one newspaper report of the period states; "*William Gibson, who stands in the market with pots, was fined at yesterday's borough sessions 2s 6d and costs, or fourteen days for shouting his wares for sale in the market contrary to the bye-laws".* Mr Gibson had probably fallen foul of one of the market officers whose job it was to ensure all market rules were adhered to, along with the additional task of collecting market tolls. The obstructing of these officers in the course of their work was in itself an offence, as too was the use of foul and abusive language towards them, as indeed was the general use of any such language anywhere in or about the market place. As had been the case with Mr Gibson, anyone in breach of the new market bye-laws would have found themselves being brought before justices of the peace and if adjudged guilty could have been fined any amount up to a maximum of £5 for each offence. As can be seen from these bye-laws the opening times for the market were 6am on weekdays and 5am on Saturdays. With such early starts it can only be guessed at what time those dealers who traded in fresh food must have begun their day. For before setting out their stalls they would have first had to travel to the market with fresh supplies of meat or fish. Indeed it would have been a long day for any trader, for the days' business did not cease until 10pm weekday-evenings and 11.30pm on Saturdays. As for those who sold items like meat, fish and poultry they were obliged to make sure certain jobs relating to cleanliness and hygiene were carried out before the close of each days trading. However, having stated this, the butchers for some reason were allowed to close at the earlier time of 8pm during the week, probably to aid them in their cleansing duties. The only days on which the market did not open were Sundays, Good Friday, Christmas Day or any days when a public fair was being held. Although even on Christmas Day and Good Friday fish was allowed to be sold until 10am in the morning.

After visiting the market and having made all their purchases the shopper now laden with any number of heavy bundles or baskets would not have relished their journey home, even if it was only the short distance to one of the nearby streets. For a few coppers they could now be relieved of this tiresome burden, as employed by the market were a number of men known as 'carriers', and were easily identifiable by a badge worn upon their right arm. As their title suggests these people would carry home any shopping for the public up to a weight of forty pounds. The scale of charges set out for this most welcome of services being one penny for every three hundred yards. The market at this time was certainly proving a good source of income for the council, for in 1853 market revenue was £560 but this had increased to £1,500 by 1866, and with an outlay during this same period of only £5,000 showed a considerable return for the money expended.

At several council meetings held towards the end of 1866 discussions regarding further improvements to the market had been taking place but without anything being officially finalised. Councillor Mills at a meeting which took place during January 1867 brought up the subject of the clock tower, enquiring that if improvements were carried out could the elevation of the clock tower be made part of the plans, for in his opinion; "*it was the best public clock in the town and if it could be better seen the public convenience would all the better be served*". According to Alderman Galt the basement of the market would not support a higher structure and to carry out Councillor Mills' suggestion would entail part of the building being pulled down. By February a resolution was finally put forward... *"that a sum not exceeding £1,800 be applied for the purpose of extending the market".* Before the resolution was voted upon several councillors voiced their opinions on several matters that were causing them some concern. One was the proposed new market to be built in Dukinfield and the one under construction in Stalybridge. It was thought the people of these towns would take advantage of their own markets as opposed to travelling to Ashton. However, it was argued that the Ashton market was regarded as having an appeal not only to local people but to those from much further afield who travelled into town by train, attracted by this first-class shopping place. If both Dukinfield and Stalybridge were building new markets, then Ashton should compete with them and go ahead with making improvements. After a lengthy debate the resolution was finally carried. The plans for these latest improvements were drawn up by John Eaton & Sons and were to include the building of an extension covering 1073 sq. yards of land on the northern side of the hall. The plans must have given much pleasure to councillor Mills for the work was also to include the elevation of the clock tower. However due to the extra work now involved the original sum of £1,800 was insufficient, and there is an agreement which has survived, dated 8th May, 1867 showing that the sum of £2,800 was to be paid to building contractor Thomas George for undertaking the work. The whole of the west frontage to the market building, facing the open market, was dismantled. The old clock spire was torn down allowing for the erection of the new clock tower. Standing at an elevation of sixty-two feet, the new tower was to be a good twenty feet higher than its predecessor

Further upheaval to what was already akin to a building site came about when during August the caravans, rides and amusements of the wakes fair came onto the market ground. The many delights and attractions that this annual event brought to town on this occasion included side shows, flying boats, exhibitions and many roundabout type rides especially of the hobby horse kind. Two such rides owned by a local man John Donnelly apparently 'took the shine out of the others'. As to which attractions were the most popular, the local paper couldn't decide between the pea-booths or the hobby horses, but did state; *"it seems impossible to have a fair or wakes nowadays without them".* With periods when the ground was overflowing with people it would appear that not only did the whole town turn out, but also many a visitor from surrounding districts. No doubt had the market ground been any larger the council would have been happy to rent it, for as it was they were already making quite a profit from charges to showmen. There is a story of one showman, who having his attraction on Ashton market, was asked by a friend; *"what do they charge you a yard here?"* Replying he said; *"yard, yard, they don't charge here by the yard, they charge you by the damned inch".*

Most of the work being carried out on the market had been completed by November 1867, and by the time of the official opening on Saturday 16th most of the new stalls, a variety of food, clothing and housewares had been occupied. The local press reported that; "*the arrangements of the crockery stalls in this new north wing were very good indeed, much surpassing the old ones in every respect*". The Roman architecturally styled appearance of the new frontage, along with the ornamental clock tower, which was finally completed in February 1868, gave to the building the look that has survived all these years and is the one we all recognise today. One of the new stallholders who moved into the extension was tripe dresser Richard Entwistle, who had founded his business in 1850 from premises on Wellington Road. Richard's great grandson Alfred said; "*after operating and building up a successful business from his shop Richard decided it would be a good move to go inside the market hall and when they advertised for tenants he duly applied*".

You may recall the old nursery rhyme; 'To *market to market to buy a fat pig. Home again home again jiggedy jig*'. It isn't hard to imagine some young child skipping along singing this, while travelling to Ashton with his or her father, perhaps even to buy that fat pig. For although the two charter fairs and four smaller ones had ceased by this time, there had developed a regular cattle market which was held on the market ground on the second Thursday of each month. Tolls charged for each animal sold varied over the years, but in 1879 they were standing at Horses...4d, Cows...2d, and Sheep...l½d the sheep pens at this time were situated on the Katherine Street side of the building. Whilst fronting the hall from Katherine Street to Bow Street were chains suspended between rows of metal posts, which were used by farmers to secure their cattle. Poorer people of the town would gather on these market days, bringing with them their pails and jugs, for many of the farmers would allow them to milk the cows and keep the milk free of charge.

The small corner of the market hall that was home to the various fish stalls had been for a good many years the cause of some consternation to councillors and public alike. It seems that the odorous smell that emanated from that portion of the hall was obviously off-putting to shoppers and not at all conducive to the attracting of trade. Even in 1867 at the time of the last market extension one councillor had asked if the fish section could be separated from the rest of the building; "*as it caused a great nuisance, especially in the summer season*". Ten years after the last major improvements had been carried out, Parliament was once again giving their approval to the Ashton Corporation's plans for further developments to the town, with the passing of another 'town improvement act'.

The Improvement act of 1877’ now enabled the council to carry out various works including the enlargement of the town hall, police offices and cells, along with extensions to the market hall. The council were now contemplating an idea for an enlargement to the market hall which was to mainly accommodate a new section for fish, poultry and game. The intended work was to be once again built along the northern, Katherine Street, side of the building. The decision to go ahead with the work was taken by the market committee in June 1880, though plans for the inclusion of cellars and ice house were dropped as they were thought too costly and unnecessary. Although the architect was instructed to prepare necessary specifications, start of work on the project seems to have been very slow. It was to be at the March committee meeting of 1881 that the town clerk gave details of the agreement he had prepared regarding the extension. He explained that it had been decided that nine months be allowed for the completion of the work and that a clerk of works should be sought with a salary of 45s a week.

CHOICE NEW VEGETABLE
AND FLOWER SEEDS.
The above to be had from
THOMAS DALE,
NURSERY SEEDSMAN,
NO. 10, MARKET HALL.
Gardens and Greenhouses kept.

Market Hall trader Thomas Dale advertising his business in 1877

ASHTON-UNDER-LYNE CORPORATION.—CLERK OF WORKS.—WANTED, a Person competent to undertake the duties of Clerk of the Market Extension Works, at a wage of £2 5s. per week.—Applications, with copies (only) of testimonials, to be sent in to the undersigned, not later than noon of Thursday, the 17th March, endorsed "Clerk of Works." Canvassing Members of the Council will disqualify.

By Order, JOHN NEAL,
Town Hall, 12th March, 1881. Borough Comptroller.

Advertisement for 'clerk of works' from the Reporter newspaper March 1881

Upon start of the building work, wooden huts were erected on the market ground, which were to temporarily house the butchers and meat traders, who because of the upheaval of the improvements had been forced from within the market hall. During the course of the building work these huts began to attract large numbers of rats and frequent rat hunts were held by the townsfolk, who with the aid of their dogs, found it an engaging pastime and was certainly one means of keeping the vermin at bay.

The design work for this new extension was once again undertaken by architects John Eaton & Sons, who had also been responsible for the last improvement to the market. It was hoped that 'William Neal' the Ashton firm of builders could complete the work by late October or early November. The commemorative granite slab inscribed 1881, which is still visible today on the wall facing the market ground, shows they succeeded.

However, a few more months were to pass before the new addition was to succumb to the hustle and bustle of the public, an event which eventually took place on Friday morning February 24th 1882. A party of sixteen council members including the Mayor Alderman Ely Andrew and the market committee chairman, Alderman James Walker, departed for the market from the town hall in procession, led by the chief constable who was acting as mace bearer. Proceeding through a market ground filled with hundreds of people the civic dignitaries entered into the new fish market. After several speeches, Alderman Walker officially declared the new section open, saying to the stallholders that he hoped they would give the public the best article for the lowest price they could possibly afford.

The fish market occupied the land that had once housed the sheep pens and was built to adjoin the 1867 extension. This now consequently brought the building on the northern side, out as far as the Katherine Street boundary. Of course refrigeration was still a good way off in 1882, and so the interior of the fish market was kept as cool as possible by the exclusion of direct sunlight, with fresh air being provided through louvered panels. The cooling effect was completed by use of enamelled bricks for which the council had allowed an extra £700. The look of the predominantly white bricked 114ft x 30ft hall was broken by a touch of decoration from two lines of light blue bricks. The stalls themselves all had Sicilian marble slabs on which the fish was kept fresh while on display. Most also had wrought iron racks from which would be hung long lines of rabbits, partridges and other game. The main stalls were the ones occupying the prominent corner positions, which also had their own offices.

1881
**This fish market
and the adjoining meat market
were erected A.D. 1881**

Building committee
Ald. Jas Walker Chairman

Councillors
Joshua Lingard, Thomas Ellison,
William Andrew, William Burgess,
Benjamin Hill, A.W. Siddall
Charles Gartside Town Clerk
William Neil Builder
John Eaton & Sons Architects
Thomas Heginbottom Esq. JP Mayor.

The wording as inscribed on the granite tablet

Through the use of matching brickwork the new extension blended well with the rest of the market building. The two new entrances both had gateways of polished stone complete with rectangular columns on either side, the tops of which had been richly carved. Each entrance also had its own pair of ornamental wrought iron gates, which had been especially designed to compliment the market and its fare. To the left of the main entrance from the market ground was a very ornate granite drinking fountain, unfortunately long gone. However, the granite tablet set into the wall to the right of the main entrance is still to be seen today. The total costs involved in the construction of the extension were approximately £6,000. With the opening of the new fish market, the old fish stalls inside the market hall were all refitted and adapted for use by other traders. The meat market now consisted of a row of stalls, or to be more correct, shops. These shops ran the full length of the hall from the market ground to Market Street and were back to back with the new fish market. Of the 115 businesses housed within the building in the late 1880s nine belonged to butchers, eight to fishmongers and a staggering seventeen to the greengrocery trade. A great variety of businesses occupied the other stalls including toy dealers, confectioners, milliners, watchmakers, tripe dressers, clothes dealers and nurserymen. One of the three nurserymen trading at this time was Ridgeway's, who had their market garden at Marple. With no direct rail route between the two towns transporting their stock to the market hall proved to be an arduous task for many years. An early start was essential

(Above): Thanks to the Improvement Act of 1887 work was soon carried out on expanding the Town Hall (right) and on erecting the Fish Market (left). (Below) The interior of the Fish Market

Just four small wheeled handcart stalls occupy the market probably for ice cream or other foodstuff.
Each has a small box on which the stallholder stood.
The various advertising signs on the market hall include those for Bovril, Livesey's Restaurant, The Empire Hippodrome and Burrows Tea Merchants.

to enable the movement of stock from their premises in Marple to the canal side, where it was loaded onto an awaiting barge. After the slow moving journey to Ashton's Portland Basin the stock was then transferred onto hand carts for the last part of the trip along the town's cobbled streets to the market hall. Perhaps one of the most unusual sights on the market ground around this time was that of the travelling dentist. He would arrive on the site on a horse drawn wagon which also served as a platform and which held his dentist's chair and a four piece band. Crowds began to gather, as standing upon his platform he would speak about dental hygiene, something to which the public at this period gave very little thought. Incidentally, there would have been many a person with bad teeth or toothache only too willing to climb aboard the wagon and take their turn in the chair. When seated the dentist would proceed to make his examination or extraction and if the patient should make any undue noise or scream the four musicians seated on the platform would instantly strike up a tune to drown out the cries.

NOAH
BESTWICK

Wholesale and Retail Butchers

Orders collected and delivered promptly

MARKET HALL
- ASHTON-UNDER-LYNE -

One of the nine butchers stalls situated in the market hall in 1888.

The diamond jubilee of Queen Victoria was a time for the country to celebrate and for the townsfolk of Ashton it was to be no exception as they gathered in their hundreds around the market place. This however, was subsequently less than had congregated ten years previously in 1887 on the occasion of her Golden Jubilee. An added attraction at that event was a flight over the town by a 90ft high gas filled balloon. The public began to arrive early in the morning as the preparations for the ascent from the market ground were still in progress. The police were out in strength and kept the people confined to the surrounding footpaths, for a good deal of the market ground itself was roped off to accommodate the ever enlarging globe. The balloon aptly named Victoria had reached its final magnitude by 1.30pm by which time the crowds looking on in awe had been allowed from the streets to fill the market ground. Lift off was delayed however, as a few adjustments had to be made. Planning to join the pilot Mr F Jackson on the flight was Isaac Watt Boulton a prominent local engineer and Mr Andrew whose first flight this was to be. However, due to problems with their combined weights it was decided that Mr Watt Boulton's son James would take the place of his father. The eventual lift off at 1.45pm was greeted by cheers of delight from the assembled thousands now surrounding the area. The market hall although not overly decorated for the occasion was nevertheless tastefully adorned with flags and colourful bunting running from the clock tower to the market roof, whilst its walls displayed the Prince of Wales feathers.

Crowds gather on the market ground in celebration of Queen Victoria's Golden Jubilee

BURROWS BROTHERS
Finest Preserves & Teas

Stall Nº 30 Market Hall
Ashton-under-Lyne

Although Stamford Street was the town's main shopping street, the shops situated on Warrington Street, Bow Street, the Market Avenue and Market Street were proving to be just as busy and added to the popularity of the market square. Taking a walk along Market Street at this time one would find a variety of shops. Starting from the Old Street end there was John Harrison the draper, who was next door to Marsden and Bradwell grocers, these two shops being on the left hand side just before Bow Street. On the opposite side directly facing the market hall was George Williamson Butcher, next door was the hardware business run by James Radcliffe where one could buy gas mantels, candles, donkey stones and brushes. Numbers 8, 10, 12, and 14, Market Street were all grocers, with shops 12, and 14, belonging to Allen Shaw who also had a provisions shop at the top of the Market Avenue. The other two grocers were William Sabine and George Wood giving a total of four similar businesses on such a short stretch of road. Moving along there was William Greenwood hairdresser, James Pownall bootmaker followed by what was a most popular shop for the period, the pawnbroking business of Samuel Broadbent. Crossing Fletcher Street the remaining business on Market Street was that of William Knowlson plumber.

Marks and Spencers are today one of the country's leading high street retailers and looking back into their early history not only do we see them forming their famous partnership in 1894, but also opening one of their stalls in Ashton market during the same year. Their 'Marks & Spencer's Original Penny Bazaar' opened in the market hall on January 20th and covered an area of 370 square feet with a frontage of 23ft. Although trading with the name 'Penny Bazaar' they did over the years sell a variety of differently priced items, but all within the price range of one-penny to one-shilling. The stall ceased trading thirty five years later on May 18th 1929.

Ashton's use of electricity as a new power source was made possible when the corporation erected their first generating plant on Wellington Road in 1897. During October of the following year a contract between the council and electrical contractors W.A. Shaw & Co. was agreed upon, for their installation of electric lighting in the public market. William Albert and Edward Arthur Shaw of Warren Street Stockport were paid the sum of £575 10s for undertaking the work. It is not known exactly how long they took to complete their task, but no doubt the market would have been among the first to receive electricity from the new plant. Two years later in September 1900 the market committee agreed that all charges for lighting in the market hall should be abolished and instead an increase of a halfpenny per foot per week being charged to each stallholder.

Marks & Spencer's Penny Bazaar opened in Ashton Market Hall in1894 and traded until 1929

Chapter Two.

To market to market to buy a plum cake,
Home again, home again ne'er a one baked;
The baker is dead and all his men,
And we must go to market again.

A market scene circa 1907 – although there is a distinct lack of stalls There nonetheless appears to be quite a large crowd of people.

During the summer months of 1900 the cotton industry was beginning to face a most difficult period and many mills had already introduced 'short time' working for their employees. Over the oncoming years this was to eventually result in an almost total decline of cotton in the town. As a result of the 'short time', the Wakes holiday of 1900 was for many, a stay at home one, with perhaps a trip to Belle Vue being a highlight for some. For most however, it was the usual annual fair on the market ground that proved to be the great attraction. The air was filled by a mixture of sounds coming forth from steam engines, big drums and organ music along with shrieks and laughter of the public as they ventured onto rides or tried their luck on the side shows. Many of the shies and shooting galleries reflected the Boar war which at this time was at its height. The exaggerated features of the South African generals De Wit, Botha, Stayn and Kruger were all used as targets for the public's enjoyment. Without a doubt one of the greatest attractions at this fair would have been the bioscope, a moving picture show which enthralled the public with short flickering images projected onto a screen. The whole market area was as always a bustling place with thousands of people being transported to the fair from surrounding districts by the tramcars of the Oldham, Ashton and Hyde Electric Tramway. Incidentally it would be another two years before trams operated by The Ashton Corporation would be introduced.

During the early 1900s other entertainments brought to the market ground were those provided by Chipperfield's, Mander's and Sedgwick's who all brought animal shows or circuses to town. These invariably included wild animals the likes of lions and tigers all rarely seen by the public outside such shows. The noise made by the animals certainly put an amount of fear into some of the public, as was related to us by Leonard Corns, a former Ashtonian now residing in Blackpool. At this period in time Leonard's father, then a young boy lived with his family at town hall chambers which stood on Katherine Street facing the market ground. His father was Doctor Corns who held his surgery within this building, adjacent to which was the Town Hall Inn which in turn was next door to Mann's Funeral parlour near to the town hall. Leonard recalls being told by his father of seeing these menageries arriving on the market. *"As youngsters my dad and his brother would watch from the window as these huge cages were pulled onto the market ground by a number of horses, the noise and activity was fascinating. "Their bedroom window overlooked the market and to be awakened in the dead of night by the ferocious roars of these animals was quite frightening. "After all, it was only the width of Katherine Street which separated them and they were really scared that the animals might escape. "It was something unusual to have animals like this so close to your home, people in those days were not used to such things".*

Original fireplace discovered still in situ after the fire of 2004

Around this time the market hall was still without any major source of heating, however there were several stalls including some of the butchers' shops, which had their own inbuilt fire places. These were put to use during the cold winter months, something which modern Health & Safety laws would not allow today. Some of the other traders in their attempts to keep their staff warm would utilise a galvanised bucket filled with hot glowing coke. It was said that cold water obtainable from a communal tap was boiled on these to make warming pots of tea. Hot water when required for cleaning purposes had to be brought over from the nearby town hall. With each of the huge wooden sliding doors of the market entrances being left wide open to the elements from morning till night, this could only have added to the problems of keeping warm, for rain, snow and especially wind would sweep through the building. As if this wasn't bad enough there was also the to generous ventilation holes in the roof which allowed in the freezing draughts and water. It was no surprise therefore that those working inside the hall would often be dressed for the great outdoors with thick woollies, scarves and heavy coats being the order of the day.

Of the many greengrocers within the market at the onset of the 1900s one was Harry Walters who became widely known to the public as Ashton's 'Banana King'. If at this time it was bananas that the shoppers wanted then Harry Walters' stall was the place to go. Unlike today where the hands (or bunches) of bananas are obtained ready boxed, Harry would obtain his supply while they were still on their stalks. Buying them by the ton he collected them from the train at Charlestown railway station. Surrounding the top of Harry's stall was a metal rail from which the many stalks of green bananas were hung to ripen. Eventually Harry moved out onto the open market with another stall, leaving the indoor business to be run by the womenfolk of the family.

During the 1880s many Italian immigrants had settled in and around Manchester and a great number of these soon established themselves in the ice cream trade. One, John Talco settled in Ashton and began to build up a growing concern. Mrs Borsey of the local butchers of that name remembers; *"When I was 11 years old in 1912, I was friendly with other shopkeeper's children and in particular with those of Hartley's outfitters who were in the Market Avenue....and to us Talco always meant 'the kokey pokey man'"*. At the time recalled by Mrs Borsey, it would have been John Talco's son who along with other relatives took over the business in 1904. The term Kokey Pokey or Hokey Pokey is believed to have originated from the Italian ice cream vendors street cry of *"Gelati Eco un Paco"*. The ice cream which was multicoloured and hard was made of a mixture of gelatine, milk and cornstarch frozen and then sliced into pieces and sold wrapped in paper. For any ice cream trader ice itself was a vital commodity and other traders who relied on ice as an important aid to their businesses were the butchers and fish mongers; these traders who without the aid of refrigeration had to use ice along with salt in order to keep their meat and fish fresh. Any meat which was not placed on display was stored in a large cabinet, on the back of which was a galvanised container holding alternate layers of ice and salt, which helped to maintain the freshness of the meat. A supplier of ice to this area was Lancashire Hygienic Dairies who transported big blocks to many businesses. Many of the butchers in the market, along with other traders in the area, who required ice, could also obtain it from a more local source... Chadwick Dam. At this time John Talco was to put to use a method of preserving ice, which he had learnt in his

The Market
from the vantage point of the Town Hall steps
Circa 1910

native Italy. Acting upon his advice ice was removed from the frozen Chadwick Dam during the winter months and then stored in an underground chamber at the rear of Stamford Park boating lake. This practice proved highly successful and provided the required ice to the traders during the warm summer months. Both John Talco and his wife Angelino, would often be seen serving on the open market ground, and a treat most popular at this time at Talco's was a 'penny lick'. This was a very small portion of ice cream in a shallow glass and to make it seem more than there was, the ice cream was brought to a peak. It gained its name because it obviously sold for one penny and upon eating the ice cream everyone licked the glass clean before handing it back. The couple retired from the ice cream trade in 1904 taking up the license of the Horse and Jockey public house in sight of the market on Wellington Road, their ice cream business did not suffer as there were other members of the family to continue the tradition.

During the first decade of the twentieth century the market had been attracting people from all walks of life. The more well-to-do folk, while picking up the odd bargain, went mainly to be entertained by the patter of the traders and the side-shows. Predominantly, though the market was being used by the poorer families – not just as a source of cheap shopping but also as a meeting place and one of recreation. The less reputable traders would make their profits selling 'questionable bargains' to this rather vulnerable sector of the public. It was the poor and unemployed that made up the crowds which thronged around the crockery stall in an attempt to buy household articles or cheap ornaments for their homes. It was the same people who purchased the thin flimsy floor coverings that passed for 'linoleum'. The 'second hand' clothing stall was also a major draw. But perhaps 'second-hand' was too good of a term for the type of clothing on sale as this description from the period relates...

The dealer in old clothes has huge hampers stacked at the back of him containing his stock-in-trade. He pulls at a shapeless looking bundle. *"This skirt; sixpence. Who'll have it? "Here".* And it is tossed into the crowd. Waiting only to deposit the proceeds safely in his hip pocket, the clothier – of the poor – dips again into his hamper. Once again, *"Who'll have it! Sixpence".* And again a voice from the crowd, whereupon the garment is tossed, without ceremony, in that direction. A youth gets it, and looks it over carefully. He may have bought things in this same way before. Then comes another lot. A child's shabby jacket is hauled from one of the hampers. Then a small pair of shoes, woefully crushed out of shape, and covered with mildew. Then another pair, and another, each in the same sorry state. One pair is badly broken. They are rolled in the jacket. *"Here, sixpence. Anyone?"* Once more a voice, a small voice, from the crowd below, and a thin, pale-faced woman stretches out her hands to catch the bundle as it falls. There is something very tragic in a woman eagerly giving sixpence for a child's old jacket and three little pairs of broken shoes. And the night was cold and raw – and the business proceeded quite uninterruptedly. 'Tis the year of our Lord nineteen hundred and eight and we are used to these things'.

A busy shopping day at Ashton Market – circa 1910

Also to be seen was the silver tongued trader, convincing people that their ailments – of any and all descriptions – could be cured by his bottles of 'mixture', and soon his stock of 'quack medicines' was being snapped up. People may not have always obtained a genuine bargain at the market but every visit would see them enjoying the sales-talk and humour of various traders. The dark and cold winter nights were just as busy as any during the summer months as crowds thronged beneath the great arc lights and the glow of the naphtha lamps. Saturday nights were the busiest times, as great numbers of people converged on the market in pursuit of bargains and the 'fun of the fair'. As the evening changed into night those trading in fresh foodstuffs, not wanting anything left on their hands over weekend, would reduce their prices dramatically – Here once again, the impoverished element of the town were to the fore. The strident tones of the traders could be heard above the noise of the crowds, but as night progressed an almost monotonous drone of music from the rides practically overwhelmed them. Occasionally the music was punctuated by the cracks from the shooting galleries and the laughter and general hubbub from the side-shows. Although far from a full scale fun fair there was still enough variety, fun and excitement to be had. Many of the showmen provided permanent fixtures on the market ground while others stayed for periods ranging from weeks to months. Roundabouts, Galloping Horses, Swing Boats, Coconut Shies, a Fire Eater, Escapologist and not forgetting the political orator all gave the market an exciting and unique atmosphere one quite different to that of the usual weekday markets.

With the market area holding such an appeal to the public and with it continuing to draw from outside of the district, anyone owning a shop in the immediate vicinity would have also built up a good trade. A typical shopping street of this time was Bow Street which offered an array of differing businesses. Starting from the Warrington Street end, these included, Travis' chip shop which reputedly sold the best chips in town and further along there was Jones Music Shop with its wide variety of musical instruments. A busy circulation office for one of the Manchester evening newspapers was also situated on Bow Street next door to Hawkins Cafe; this cafe was a popular choice for the market traders as well as the public. At the corner of the Market Avenue was the business of a most well respected trader, Allen Shaw's provisions shop. In offering to wrap the customers purchases Mr Shaw, in his rather distinctive voice, would always ask; *"would you like a little bit of brown paper".* On the opposite corner was the shop of butcher, T. Coop which was adjacent to the public house The New Market Inn, owned by the Openshaw Brewery and run at this time by Mary Carr. Housewives at this period did a lot of home baking and providing for their needs was the Flour Shop of Allen Shaw a single storey building next to the inn. The terminus and office for the City of Manchester's

T. Coop Family Butcher (left) with Allen Shaw's provisions shop opposite (right).

trams stood next door, this rest room was also used by the drivers of Ashton's trams too. At the end of the street there was situated Page's Chemist; Mr Page was a well known character with a rather pointed bald head, and, being self conscious about this, he could often be seen wearing a hat. After serving members of the public Mr Page would in a tuneful voice always say; *"I thank yooo!"* as they left his shop. Just on the corner, between Bow Street and Old Street, was Livesey's Restaurant. This establishment was, no doubt a popular port of call for many a hungry

A view of the market reproduced from a postcard dated 1913.

shopper; most of who looked on as 'Owd Livesey', as he was affectionately known, carved the meat in full public gaze in the window. For many years the walls of the market hall carried various advertising panels, including several for this popular restaurant.

The Market Hall can be seen in the background with Livesey's Restaurant on the left

At the start of the First World War conscription had still to be introduced, but a soon to be familiar sight in town and especially on and around the market, was the army band whose playing of stirring military tunes raised the patriotic spirits within the young men. Encouraged by their friends usually female, these young men were soon with the recruiting officer and were signing up to serve their country; many of course were under age but were accepted none the less. The effects of the war were felt in the town in more ways than one.

In the markets this was noticeable by the absence of many of the menfolk who had gone to fight. Some stalls closed altogether because of this, whilst others were run by older men or those unfit to fight, but in the main it was the women and young girls who kept the businesses going. A shortage of goods made it extremely difficult for the market and its traders, and those dealing in the meat business suffered particularly badly.

Borsey's Butchers which was situated on Old Street traded well, right up to the 1980s, and looking back 91 year old Mrs Borsey recalled the war years; *"You simply couldn't get hold of beef at all, pigs were a little easier to obtain though not always so. We had our own slaughter house at the rear of the shop and from the pigs, besides their meat, we could make such things as black puddings, savoury ducks, sausages and dripping.*

When we had these items for sale we would put a notice up to inform the people, just like they did over at the market, and before you knew it queues were forming, you see people were just glad to get hold of whatever they could. "As we had our own slaughter house we also supplied other butchers, and I remember having to take sausages into the market on a number of occasions and in there the butchers, just like us, had the problem of what to wrap the meat up in. You see even paper was hard to get, and because of the shortage customers were asked by stallholders and shops to bring their own paper with them. I remember one butcher in particular, getting quite annoyed with one of his customers, the poor woman hadn't brought any paper and was visibly shaking when the butcher, fuming as he was, slammed down his big knife on the wooden table and bellowed out for all to hear; 'if you can't bring any paper you could at least bring two plates to put the meat between, don't you know there's a war on'. I don't think he really meant to be as hurtful as he sounded."

Newspapers were used for wrapping goods for many years – and were readily available as this advertisement from 1920 shows - However, during the war years it was a different matter with newsprint being in short supply.

Bailey's which had been established in the market since 1852 selling toys, had by this time expanded and a second stall had been acquired for a hardware business, both were now being operated by Jim Bailey, grandson of the founder. Harvey Wright who started working for Bailey's in 1915 as a young boy, recalls; "*My brother Harold who worked for Jim Bailey came home with a message on Christmas eve, asking if I could go an errand for Mr Bailey, so off I went to his stall. "On my arrival the market was absolutely packed solid with people, and although there was very little money to be had at this time, people had obviously scrimped and saved, and so, being Christmas you can imagine what business a toy stall was doing. I stood around waiting to discover the nature of my errand when a number of people began to question me about some of the toys, asking their prices. "I asked Mr Bailey just what he wanted of me and his reply was to forget the errand and to serve the people. I did as he said and stayed until the end, in those days the market didn't close until 11pm and upon cashing up he asked me how I had enjoyed it. Smashing I said, so there and then he offered employment, which I took up and started a few days later. I was only 10 years old and obviously still at school, but I still worked everyday during the school dinner time, and after school I went straight to the stall starting at 4.50pm through till 8pm. On Saturdays I had to be there for 8.15am to take off the stall covers and I finished work at 9pm, all this work was for a wage of 4s 6d a week".* Another person who

W. MOSS.

Tinplate Worker.
Hardware, Brushes,
and General Dealer.

Mats and Brushes in great variety.

A large assortment of fuel economisers always in stock.
All classes of tinware made to order.

3 & 4 Market Hall
ASHTON-UNDER-LYNE.

Mr Moss founded his business in the years preceding the Great War. Although under different ownership the stall still occupied the same position until the fire of 2004 worked inside the market hall at this period was Ivy Jackson, now Mrs Ivy Robinson, she says; *"I started to work for Fay Reimer on her ribbon stall in 1916, I worked from 9am till 8pm, except for Tuesdays when I finished at 1pm, my wage for this was £1 per week. During my time on this stall the lady who ran the millinery business next door, Mrs Hall, had been watching me work and began to try and persuade me to work for her. As an inducement she offered me an extra 5s on top of what I was then earning, this was a lot of money, so I asked Fay Reimer if she could match the offer, she couldn't so I moved over to Mrs Hall. "Apart from when the war brought bad news I do recall that the market was a very happy place to work in, it was a time of course when everyone helped each other."*

Perhaps the most tragic news from the war years for Ashton-under-Lyne was when a local munitions factory - The Hooley Hill Rubber and Chemical Co - exploded killing 46 people and injuring hundreds more. The effects of the blast were felt in all the surrounding towns and even up to twenty miles away. On Sunday June 17th 1917, a public funeral service was held on the market ground for 13 of those who had perished in the disaster. The market square presented a sombre scene as the 13 horse drawn hearses and 50 mourning coaches lined up in front of the town hall, with the rest of the market ground being thronged with hundreds of people all paying their last respects.

Sombre scene on the market ground as a public funeral service is conducted for some of those who died in the munitions explosion.

It was in 1920 that young Ivy Jackson left Mrs Hall's employment. *"During my time with her"*, said Ivy, *"She had married again; her husband was now Mr Robinson who ran a nursery stall at the other end of the market hall. Well, Mrs Robinson as she now was had a drink problem and her husband was aware of this, and told the staff that if anyone ever went to get whisky for her, then he would sack them. In turn Mrs Robinson herself said to me, that if I refused to go for her whisky then she would sack me. I was in a no win situation. So one day I went for her whisky and was found out by Mr Robinson who promptly gave me the sack. It didn't seem to be long after this event that they gave up their businesses in the market, which to my mind just came about by her drink problems".*

In July 1920 the market cafe which had been owned for a good many years by Mrs Nancy Hawkins was taken over by Susanna Finnerty, bringing to the market a name and business that was to remain right up to the 1990's.

Forty years had now gone by without any significant changes having been carried out to the market hall, and the market committee in 1921 hoped to be able to make use of an allotted £11,000 for improvements. However, whatever plans they had, had to be dropped when government approval was not forthcoming - it was to be a further eight years before any work was to commence.

Horse drawn carrier outside Town Hall Chambers near to Market Ground at the junction of Warrington Street and Katherine Street.

Very few market people had their own transport in these days and many would travel to town by rail. Shim Kay one of many traders who came from Manchester's Jewish community, would put his large skip onto the train at Victoria station arriving in Ashton shortly after 9am. Leonard Corns recalled working for Shim Kay, when only a boy aged about eight years: *"I would be waiting every Saturday at Charlestown station for this train to arrive, many traders were on board, Mr Kay and I would wheel the skip on a hand truck along Warrington Street towards the market, where I would then unpack it for him".* Shim Kay was, like his father-in-law Harry Gilbert, a jeweller and sold pocket watches. Mr Corns continued; *"I enjoyed myself and he paid me 2s 6d which was a lot of money. Some people were working for £2 a week, so 2s 6d to a lad of eight was a lot. The market was open from 9am until late at night, although they weren't continually trading all the time, there were flat spots which were from 12.30pm to 2.30pm then again from 4.30pm to around 6.30pm when the busy night time trading would begin".*

These Saturday nights were a phenomenon of Ashton's market, over many years, for in the days before refrigeration, stallholders dealing in perishable goods, would dispose of it at greatly reduced prices. It is uncertain when they first started to do this, but as the market was open until 11.30pm on Saturday nights in 1852, it is probably safe to assume that this practice had been carried out then, and may well have started even earlier. It was certainly the 'happening' at the start of the 1900s and was still a Godsend to the unemployed and poor during the lean years of the 1920s. Throughout this time the market place on Saturday nights was thronged with people, and their visits became not just shopping trips but were also a source of cheap entertainment. In most instances the whole family would be together and many an hour would be spent listening to the humorous banter of the stallholders, while if there was a copper or two to spare there were a number of amusements and sideshows to be enjoyed. The crowds would start to gather about 7pm with many looking around at the stalls, but at this moment few were buying, instead they were waiting for that magic time when the auctions would begin, usually around 9pm. The sales pitches used by the stallholders were entertainment in themselves. 'Sam the pot man' was well known for his style in patter, and for many a year was a great source of amusement, as crowds would stand enthralled by his showmanship. Children dragged their parents to watch Mr Podmore boiling his sugar to make sweets, attracted by the sweet smelling aromas that filled the air. Their smiling faces never straying from the man, who would delight them by pulling and stretching his toffee, plaiting it like rope before cutting it into stripy minty humbugs. Can I mum? Can I? You can almost hear their cries. Of course it wasn't just the children who indulged in Podmore's sweets, many an adult walked away with a bag of toffee or butterballs secreted upon their person. Harry Gilbert stood at his stall near to the town hall, and always had large crowds to see him auction off his pocket watches. Only good things have ever been said of this man. There was Brimlow's who sold herbal medicine. He too would always attract a large crowd who were fascinated by the drawings he produced of the human body. He could draw any part of the anatomy upon a blackboard, whilst describing it as he went along, giving explanations as to how his medicines could be beneficial. Over the years he obtained a good name for his medicine and after leaving the market he continued in business from a shop on Warrington Street. An elderly lady, Mrs Dagnall we believe, operated a similar business from one of the three wooden lean-to type huts affixed to the Bow Street side of the market hall. These huts opened

Bow Street and the lean-to stalls against the market hall

up at the front and the proprietor would serve from inside. Of the others, one was for the sale of fish and oysters with the third offering tripe. Tripe was a very popular dish during this period and was not only bought to take home for a meal, but was often eaten there and then at any number of the tripe stalls. Probably the best known of these being Entwistle's, where tripe was offered already cut up on plates ready to eat for 2d or 3d. Black puddings, too, were a great favourite and it seems as though there had always been a black pudding stall on the market. Again this delicacy was more often than not consumed on the spot, picked straight out of the boiling water by the stallholder, it was instantly placed on a fresh muffin, sliced and garnished with mustard. It was indeed very popular with most Saturday night shoppers and also the late night revellers leaving the nearby public houses. The savoury duck and muffin stall and Betty Ingham's Pea-Saloon were two others frequently patronised by the hungry crowds. However, it was cheap food for the family that was the priority, as Mrs Sales in her 87th year recalled; *"I was sent to the market with a big bag to get cauliflower leaves for the 'rabbits', and I was always reminded not to let on that I was one of the 'rabbits', mother would then boil them up as cabbage for us all. I was also given a few coppers to buy some dark bananas, the brown soft ones. I got about twenty or so for the money, so it would be bananas on bread, bananas and custard or banana cake, you name it and it contained bananas. We might not have had much money but Saturday nights, were nights to treasure".* Salthouse's fruit stall would certainly have attracted attention as Jimmy Salthouse amused everyone with his spiel, as he filled up brown paper bags with apples, oranges and the like, topping it all off with a bunch of bananas all for the price of 1s. Meat, fish and bread were among the other main items on the shopping lists, and all could be picked up cheaply. Oldfield's in the market hall would offer a

Advertisement from 1920: Parkinson's was another business that would sell off its surplus stock cheaply on Saturday nights

'cracked' loaf for 1d or 2d, Alan Bincliffe and Brierley's fish stalls amongst others, would sell cheap 'wrap-ups' to clear their stocks; whilst the row of butchers in the market would compete with each other in auctioning off their remaining meat. Most of the best cuts had been sold throughout the day, but a half rabbit could be obtained for 3d, and as John Walters, son of 'Banana King' Harry Walters, recalled; *"When I was about eight years old my dad would give me 2s and send me over to get a piece of meat. He would already have seen the piece he wanted, so I would have to go early and keep my eye on it, sometimes waiting an hour or more until they finally auctioned it off. For 2s you could get a piece of meat that would last a family of six or eight people two or three days".*

The market area throughout the years has seen quite a number of characters, and one who made his presence felt; especially on Saturday nights was 'Father Muck King'. It seemed as though everyone knew 'Father', who incidentally acquired his name through selling manure to the market gardeners on Ashton Moss and to many residents of the district, but it was his Saturday night strolls around the market where he gained his friendship of the people. Very few townsfolk knew his real name, but 'Father' born John Smith was never worried by that, and enjoyed life as the 'Muck King'. His home was a court off Penny Meadow nicknamed 'Ticklebelly Alley' only a short walk from his market kingdom. He was an instantly recognisable character with his familiar long coat complete with a sprig of heather in the buttonhole. His famous red waistcoat from which would hang a gold watch chain, and the ever present gaiters over his trousers. Aided by a walking cane he really enjoyed strolling around drawing the public's attention relishing every minute of it. He would visit many of the stallholders and happily join in with their banter, on one occasion while approaching Salthouse's greengrocers stall, Jimmy Salthouse shouted out to him 'have you sold all your muck yet'. To which 'Father' replied, 'aye lad, an ave just come round t'see thee sell thine'. The jeweller Harry Gilbert was always happy to see 'Father' at his stall, telling him, 'he was always as welcome as the flowers in spring'. In some respects 'Father'

'Father Muck King', certainly one of the town's most eccentric of characters

Two contrasting pictures of Ashton Market ground during the 1920s.

The ABOVE: was obviously taken on a busy market day. While BELOW; with just a few stalls and the market hall seemingly closed could indicate this scene was captured on a Tuesday the traditional early closing day.

could have been classed as a likable rogue, for it was once said that he purloined a heavy blacksmiths anvil from a workshop, and even got the workers to help him lift it onto his muck cart. Later a policeman suspecting that something about the pile of manure just didn't seem right, stopped 'Father' to question him, and soon discovered the anvil amidst the steaming manure. Upon being asked how the anvil happened to be in the cart, 'Father' replied 'it must ave got caught up on't fork'. Young children were especially fond of following 'Father' around the market on Saturday nights, for every so often he would throw pennies their way. When the nights began to draw in, various lamps were hung from the stalls to give light, some just burnt naked flames whilst others used acetylene gas or naphtha oil; the smells from these filled the night time air with a most distinctive odour. Many of the stallholders would have hired their lamps from the local family concern of Seldon's, who were originally showpeople but who over the years were to build up a good business supplying traders with not only these lamps but also stalls. After the end of the days trading, the lamps obtained from Seldon's were collected from the market by hand carts or 'light carts' as they were known. These carts were kept near to the fish market and at the close of day they would be stored in the passage between the market hall and its Warrington street entrance. With very few of the outdoor stalls having any form of heating, it was just a matter of wrapping up well to keep out the winter elements. It would no doubt have been the female stallholders that felt the cold the most, for there was no such thing as trousers for women in those days. Leonard Corns again recalls; *"As much as I enjoyed myself I was never keen on the cold weather. After some cold days, especially if Shim Kay had had a good day, he would often say, come on lad we've just got time to have a chippy supper. He would take me over to Knight's chip shop on Warrington Street and buy me fish and chips, so I'd had a good day, a good supper, good money and even enjoyed myself".*

Besides the entertainment that had been provided by the stallholders there were also the various types of amusements and rides, which over the years had helped to make for fun filled Saturday nights. These attractions were hugely popular with children and adults alike and indeed many were aimed primarily at the adults. Plenty of enjoyment would have been received from amongst others, roundabouts, an aunt sally, kiddies swing boats, but perhaps the amusements to bring back most memories would be the two huge swing boats. These steam driven swings each carried about twenty people, all shouting with delight as the large boats swished loudly passed each other. Budding footballers made their way to the 'shoot 'em ins' where for a copper or two they would attempt to kick a football past a young lad into the net.

A time of year looked upon with mixed feelings by the market traders was the upheaval of the market ground to allow for the annual wakes fair to take place. All the stalls were cleared from the market square and re-sited on both sides of Market Street, and the one side only of Bow Street. Some traders didn't like this move, but most found trade was increased as the crowds flocked to the fair. A normal market was held on Monday, but by 9am the following day every stall had been cleared as the market superintendent commenced marking out the positions which the various sideshows and rides would occupy. Many of the showmen would have arrived in town on the Monday, being parked-up on Sackville Street near to Charlestown railway station, awaiting the big pull-on which usually commenced at around 10.30am on Tuesday and continued into Wednesday. Eventually the whole area was transformed and the fair was ready to open by Thursday afternoon. Popular attractions of the wakes fair from the mid 1920s onwards were Greens Golden Dragons which always occupied a position next to Pat Collins' Whale Island Scenic which consisted of large carriages in the form of whales which travelled around an undulating track. John Collins provided two extremely well patronised rides with his Four Abreast and the Steam Yachts. Hibbert's Jumping Horses, the Wall of Death, Dodgem Track and the Cake Walk were other big attractions which

A sight long gone – Ashton's wakes week fair occupying the market ground

always proved popular as too did the smaller Roll-a-Penny and Coconut Shies. The steam traction engines used to generate the electricity and power to drive the machines were all sited along the nearby streets. There were five on Bow Street, four or five on Katherine Street and three at the bottom of the market ground itself. These engines produced a great deal of smoke, steam and noise, but all this added to the atmosphere, making it something special for those who could not afford to holiday away. The fair was in operation on Thursday, Friday, Saturday, Monday and Tuesday, but during this final day much of the fancy decorative work would have been dismantled in readiness for a quick pull down that night. For some time it was a regular event during wakes week for the unfortunate people from the workhouse to be given the opportunity of visiting the fair ground on its final afternoon. Henry Diston, Ashton's chief constable was the inspiration behind this, having arranged with the showmen for them to provide free rides, and for market traders to give ice cream, sweets and bags of fruit. Police officers, including those that were off duty, were present to assist members of the party, which ranged from the young to the very elderly, on and off the machines. Although the rides were operated at a much slower speed than normal, they still provided a thrilling afternoon for everyone. To finish off their memorable day a visit to the nearby Queens Cinema was also arranged.

Since its transformation into a shopping thoroughfare the 'Market Avenue' had proved to be popular with the townsfolk and its variety of shops provided an ideal link between busy Stamford Street and the market ground. A walk along the Avenue from Stamford Street in 1929 would have taken you passed Lumb's fancy goods shops at numbers 5 and 35, while the Umbrella shop at number 7 seems to have belonged to the same family. A Marion Lumb also owned the milliners business at number 31 and B. Wallis owned a similar outlet at number 22. Gentlemen would have taken interest in the tailor's establishments belonging to D. Pickering and Barlows, while J. Ridgeway and A. Butterworth's premises were gents outfitters. Those with a sporting desire would have been impressed by the display of goods within S. Harrison's sports outfitters. Tea merchants Burrows Brothers and Walker & Co were among a number to be found in the town at this period and the avenue also contained an ever popular fish mongers under the name of F. Woolven. Numbers 23 and 27 housed drapery concerns belonging to Roebuck and Wallis respectively, while the two hairdressers W. Greenwood and Wallwork's also competed for the public's custom. Before reaching Bow Street and the market, one would have passed a number of other shops and businesses including J. Bloomfield optician, E. Jones tobacconist, H. Cope & Son jewellers and watchmaker and the office of Lindley & Gibson architects.

Since its reconstruction into a shopping thoroughfare the Market Avenue continued its popularity with the townsfolk

Further Reductions in the Price of Foodstuffs

AT

MORRISONS

MARKET HALL, ASHTON-UNDER-LYNE

VERY BEST PURE LARD	7½d. per lb.
FINEST DANISH BUTTER	1/8 „
BEST FINE WHITE SUGAR	4lbs. 9½d.
WHOLE or HALF HAMS, The best in the Town	1/- per lb.
SLICED AT	1/6 „
LARGE TINS SWEETENED MILK	2 Tins 5½d.
FINEST IRISH ROLL BACON	1/6 per lb.
FINEST DANISH ROLL BACON	1/4 „
FINE LEAN MILD CURED ROLL BACON	1/- „

Large tins BARTLET PEARS, in heavy syrup, 1s. per tin.	Large tins PINEAPPLE CHUNKS or SLICES, 5½d. per tin.	Large tins PRAWNS, 7½d. per tin.

Fine Large Californian Prunes - 6d. per lb. 2lbs. 11½d.

Splendid SULTANAS 4½d. per lb.	Very Best Golden SULTANAS, 7d. lb. Sold elsewhere at 10d. lb.	Choice Cleaned CURRANTS, 6d. per lb.	Finest Quality Cleaned CURRANTS 7d. per lb.

SPECIAL OFFER. RASPBERRY & APPLE JAM, STRAWBERRY & APPLE JAM 2 lb. size 8d. 1 lb. size 4½d.	TRY THIS FRUIT PARCEL. 1 tin PEARS. 1 tin PEACHES. 1 tin APRICOTS. 1 tin CHERRIES. 1 tin PINEAPPLE CHUNKS or SLICES. 1 packet CUSTARD POWDER 1 pint TABLE JELLY, And a CARRIER BAG. THE LOT 3s.	SPECIAL OFFER. Finest WHOLE FRUIT, RASPBERRY, STRAWBERRY or BLACK CURRANT JAM, 2 lb. size, 1s. 1d. 1 lb. size, 7½d.

Princes LOBSTER. Small tins 1s. Large tins 1s. 8½d.	Libby or Morris LUNCH TONGUES, Small tins 1s. Large tins 1s. 8d.	Finest Quality DAMSON JAM, 2 lb. size 1s. 1 lb. size 7d.	Finest RED SALMON, 1 lb. tins 1s.
Best WAX CANDLES, 3 lbs. 10d. 36 Candles.	Best TAPERS, Thick or Medium, 1 lb. packets 1s.	PARAFFIN MATCHES, Strike anywhere. 8½d. per doz.	SAFETY MATCHES, 7d. per doz.

Try our Special Blends of Teas at 1/- and 1/2 per lb.

Check out these prices – The advertisement dates from 1929

Chapter Three.

To market, ride the gentlemen,
So do we, so do we;
Then comes the country clown,
hobbledy gee, hobbledy gee.

Ashton Market Hall showing the 1930 improvements

As the 1920s were rapidly reaching their end many of the local shops in the Market Avenue, Bow Street, Warrington Street and others surrounding the market place had been modernised and re-fronted. This was something that was no doubt in the minds of the market committee as they now contemplated a new look to the market hall. Having had their previous improvement plans rejected by the government in 1921 they now believed the time was right for this to finally go ahead. It was decided that the whole of the hall needed re-roofing along with a restructuring of the Bow Street and Market Street sides of the building. Plans for this work were drawn up by architects John Eaton and Sons, who had been established in Ashton for more than 100 years. This would be the third occasion on which they were to work on the market hall. At the time of the earlier projects in 1867 and 1880/81 John Eaton snr had headed the company while at this time John Eaton jnr had taken over the reigns. Another local firm, James Green builders and contractors were employed to carry out the actual construction at a cost of over £10,000. Although this proposed work would considerably alter the exterior appearance of the hall many of the market tenants were not entirely happy, feeling instead that work should have been concentrated on the interior.

John Eaton senior had originally been a stone mason; taking up architecture later, and although his sons were also architects, stonemasonry was also something they had learnt. This would probably account for the inclusion of much ornamental stonework in their projects. The stone entrances to the fish market with their rich carvings are fine illustrations of their earlier work. In this latest venture examples of John Eaton Junior's penchant for stone work are featured above the Bow Street corner entrances and middle doors and again high above the central door on Market Street. Among the decorative splendour can be seen vines and grapes along with Ashton's coat of arms. Other stonework so often overlooked by the public today, but which caused some controversy at the time are the six stone lions that sit proudly on top of the market hall. When these creatures first appeared, during early March 1930, it seemed as if everyone was more than aware of there presence. It is thought that the original design for the rooftop ornamentation was to be urns, but this brought objections from a number of market committee members who thought they would be rather gloomy and funereal. None of them however, seems to have accepted responsibility for the change in arrangement that brought the lions to the hall. Should you find yourself with a moment to spare next time you are on the market square take a look up towards these animals, and ask yourself were some of the comments made shortly after their appearance justified or not. *"They look just like monkeys". They are more like dog Toby than lions, they only want Punch and Judy to make them complete". "Ave cut better lions wi' mi' pick out ot' coal face".* One trader however, commented, *"If they create interest and bring people to Ashton I don't care if they are upside down".* Other features created at this time included a number of stained glass windows each capturing a part of the market's history. One depicted a medieval seller of pots whilst another pictured the granting of a royal charter.

On Wednesday September 24th 1930 a large crowd gathered at the town hall steps to hear Ashton's MP Mr A Bellamy and the Mayor and Mayoress Mr and Mrs Alderman Wild make speeches of gratitude, before moving

September 1930.

An eager crowd await the opening of the new market hall extension, a ceremony performed by Ashton's Mayor Alderman J. Wild

Top Left.
One of the ornamental lions which caused much attention at the time of their erection.

Middle Left.
The Ashton coat-of-arms is featured above the Market Street Entrance.

Bottom Left.
One of the stained glass windows – this a medieval seller of pots

Bottom Right.
The Wellington Road entrance showing clearly the early work of Eaton's.

over to and declaring the market hall officially open. Mr Bellamy felt that the ceremony had been a most historical one, and went on to say, *".... when Ashton ceases to be the market town of the district it will cease to be a progressive town".* However, Mr Bellamy's words were not received with much enthusiasm from several stallholders, as they believed with trade being in the doldrums; Ashton could soon cease to be a market town. This would be backed up by the Market Traders' Association, who noted that even after the council had spent large sums of money on the hall trade continued to drop. They were also unhappy about the situation within the hall stating, *"The present condition of the Market Hall is such that had it been a workshop it would have been condemned long ago".* At this period throughout the country many people were suffering due to the great depression or 'slump' as it was more commonly known. Ashton was of course no exception and many local people found themselves out of work and impoverished. Consequently, no matter how many improvements were made to the market, if people still did not have money to spend then trade would inevitably dwindle.

It was shortly after the 1930 market improvements had been completed that a young David Conn started working in the hall as a butcher's boy for Sam Whittam. Apart from a break for war service David spent all his working life in the butchery business and by talking with him we gained an insight to the market during these years. Whittam's whose rent at this

David Conn pictured in the 1950s. David started work in the market around 1932 and retired after the devastating fire of 2004.

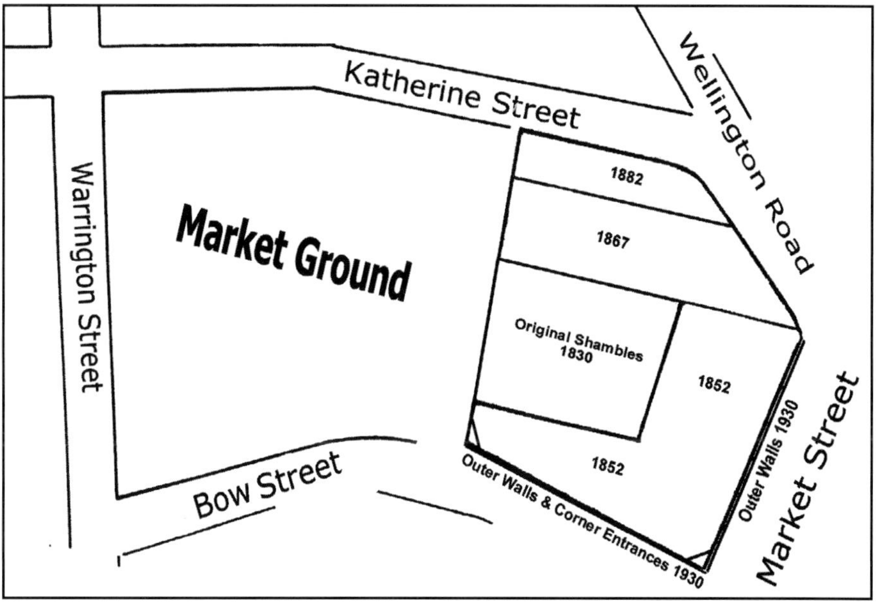

Above: ***Plan showing the various enlargements to the market hall. 1930 brought the fifth addition, with the erection of the new exterior wall on Market Street and Bow Street.***

Below: Ashton Market Hall after the 1930 improvements.

period was 10s a week was just one of many butchers, others who were apparently not just competitors but also friends, included Schofield's, Stephen's, Ashworth's, Kershaw's, J. Arda and Bill Briggs, although Kershaw's it seems, only traded on Fridays and Saturdays. Looking back David remembered that unlike today the butcher would not serve from inside the stall but instead carried out all his business from the front. With no such thing as Formica or stainless steel all the tables and working surfaces were made of wood, thus making the all important job of cleaning up a much more tedious task he recalled. When David took up employment in the market the butchers were still all slaughtering the animals themselves, *"You could go to a local farm buy a cow walk it back through the streets of Ashton right to the slaughterhouse",* said David. There was of course no refrigeration at this time so large blocks of ice were used to keep meat fresh.

Sowerbutt's along with Bradley Ibbotson were names well known to garden enthusiasts of the area for many years, and both had good businesses in the market hall as well as being acclaimed market gardeners. The name of Sowerbutt's in years to come was to gain further recognition as Bill Sowerbutt shared his knowledge through the BBC's 'Gardeners Question Time' and several newspapers including the Oldham Chronicle. The practice of taking knives to be sharpened is not one carried out regularly by many people today. However, at this period it was a service well catered for by cutler T. Smith. He also provided a vast array of cutlery from full services to single items for use in the home and also larger items for use by traders including butchers, fishmongers and restaurateurs.

Two of the many Market Hall businesses advertising their wares in the 1930s. The A.C.S. was the Ashton Co-Operative Society

It was said that Mr Smith would spend most of the day seated upon a high stool, from which vantage point he was able to see if his wife was approaching the stall. For, being a bit of a gambler, when not actually doing any business, he would use his free time scrutinising the newspaper's racing form in the hope of finding a winner. Obviously something of which

A 1930s non-market day scene with just a few stalls to the right of the market hall. Note the closed roundabout and sideshow and also the Manchester tram.

Mrs Smith would have disapproved. Miss E Hadfield was another trader who spent a good deal of time sitting, for while manning her stall she would spend many an hour trying to solve crossword puzzles and on occasions, would seem most annoyed to be disturbed by a customer. For a good many years Hadfield's stall remained well patronised by the older generations who still required the old Lancashire red flannel and spotted red hankies. Other stalls around the market hall included Fred Nuttall's cheeses, Harry Warhurst's 2d second hand book stall, Elton's opticians, Star Stores, John Moss ironmongers and Browns gent's outfitters. One particular stall which had been trading since 1910 was that of Thomas Young, suppliers of bacon, ham, cheese and preserves. Compare some of Young's prices of the early 1930s with those you would expect to pay today. Finest Danish middle cut sliced bacon 1s 2d, Danish gammon 1s 6d, Lancashire and Cheshire cheeses 1s, two pounds of blackcurrant jam 9½d, twenty ounce jar of pickles 5½d and pint jellies at just 2d.

The early 1930s also saw the market hall stallholders now provided with boiling water for cleaning and to make tea, but a charge of a half-penny was levied by the council for this privilege. Several traders also got together and paid 3d or so to a young lad, who would carry the water to their respective stalls. It was also at this period that the fish market tenants asked the Market Committee to supply them with disinfectant on a daily basis to enable them to keep the fish market in a condition which would encourage people to shop there without being met by obnoxious smells.

With the 1930s slump continuing general trade for many tenants within the market hall was not encouraging. At one meeting between tenants and the Market Committee traders complained that they had not been consulted on any expenditure spent on the hall. Also, they had seen their rents increased several times in the past and this along with the present decline in trade had been very much felt in the market hall. A rent reduction did eventually come during 1934; however, the Tenants Association's reply to this was *"We deeply regret that the decision taken by the Market Committee is to reduce the rents by only 7½%. Having had our rents increased from 33% to 50% and having proved that we are doing considerably less business today than at the time the increase was enforced, we consider that the proposed reduction shows an entire lack of sympathy with, and understanding of our present position".*

At this same period there was also a tide of discontent coming from a number of stallholders on the outside market. The situation here was that up to this point all traders had to pay the council 6s to stand the ground with some traders paying the council 1s extra to rent a stall. Several traders especially those of longstanding of ten years or more were allowed to have their own stalls at no extra cost; while the rest of the traders rented stalls for 2s from Mr Seldon. However, the council in an effort to bring some sort of uniformity to the situation, and to prevent them from having to employ workers to specifically clear away stalls, decided to hand over the management of their stalls to Mr Seldon. Consequently, Mr Seldon now had the responsibility of renting *all* stalls and of their clearance at the end of the day. However, those who had previously rented from the council now saw their charges doubled to 2s. Although the rent increase was not going in to the coffers of the council, this did not stop the traders from laying the blame squarely at their door. As an effect of this there was a protest and boycott on Monday June 19th 1933. Mr J. Sutcliffe, a spokesman for the protesters advised stallholders not to pay the increase in rent, adding that the Market Superintendent, Mr Jessie Lowe had recently had a wage increase and traders, especially in these times of poor trade should not bear the burden. Another tenant stated that it was the action of the market committee in allowing an individual (Mr Seldon) to let stalls instead of the corporation that had resulted in council workers losing their jobs.

Brothers Jack & Matt Swan at their 1930s Greengrocery stall were at this time like others on the outdoor market feeling some discontent

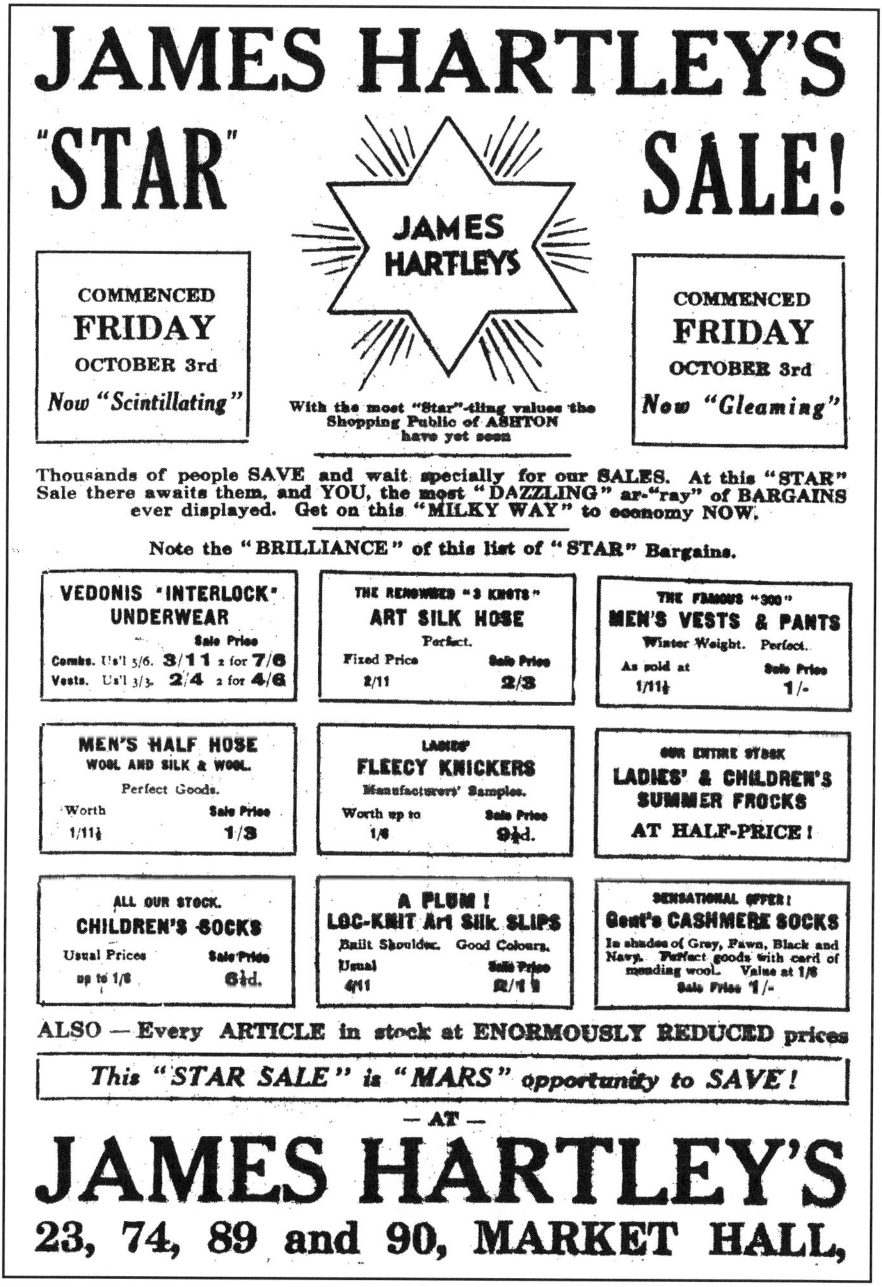

By 1936 James Hartley had outlets in twelve towns including four in Ashton's Market Hall. Their stated policy was to sell only consistently reliable merchandise at very competitive prices

The outside market at this period was trading three days a week on Monday, Friday and Saturday. Each day had a different feel for customers, even though many traders would be present on all three days. A very popular Monday stall was that which sold cooked sheep hearts and roast pork, which the trader had spent all day Sunday preparing. 'Queenie' whose name is still remembered by many of the older generation, was one of a number of traders who did not actually have a stall, but instead utilised the ground by spreading out a large tarpaulin sheet, upon which she would display her stock of ladies wear. Curtain Mary was another female stall holder who made a name for herself with some interesting and amusing patter; *"I could sell curtains better at the cemetery gates than here"*. Saturdays were of course still very busy days as far as the stallholders were concerned, and the late night shopping which had proved so popular during the past continued to draw crowds, expanding the traders day. The reason for this success remained as ever, cheap food and a cheap form of entertainment for the whole family. Traders like Podmore, Gilbert, Entwistle and others of long standing had their regular customers and knew many of them by name. A Saturday night market in the 1930s had not changed much, now instead of Jimmy Salthouse selling off cheap fruit it was Jack Swan or perhaps the proprietors of two largest greengrocery stalls at this time Percy Wright and Jack Taylor. The cost of their cheap bags of fruit though had risen to 2s or 2s 6d as opposed to the 1s or so charged by their predecessors. The crowds leaving the nearby public houses would more often than not head for the usual pitch of the young man who sold fresh chickens and eggs. Although having sold most of his stock earlier in the day he could almost guarantee they would buy any bird which he still had left on his hands. Several market traders had the use of motorised transport some of which drove directly onto the market ground and conducted business from their vehicles. Bob Fish who sold oil cloth from the back of his van, is one person remembered by many. The oil cloth would be unrolled for all to view and then Bob would go into his auctioneering routine. Many of the town's unemployed men would mingle in amongst Bob's crowds hoping to persuade the purchasers of the oil cloth, into allowing them to carry the bulky rolls home for them, at a price of course. 'The Umbrella Man' was another who traded from his vehicle and became a popular character with his quick-witted patter and display of tricks performed with the brollies, a real crowd pleaser. Eighty-one year old Miss Nellie Carter who regularly visited the market from her Bardsley home recalled; *"I think it was in the 20s that I first saw 'The Umbrella Man' on Ashton's market but it was when I was a little older in the 30s that a lasting impression was made. From beneath an open umbrella held high above his head keeping off the rain, often none existent, he would greet the crowd." "'Hello you good people of Ashton', he cried, 'Many of you will shortly be glad you stopped here today. For the discernible ones amongst you will have the good sense to purchase one of these fine umbrellas from the vast array available'; At this stage he'd turn around and point towards the back of his van, where from a number of small compartments could be seen the protruding umbrellas. 'For the next few days are going to be some of the wettest for some time, any time now the heavens will open. 'The choice is yours', he'd proclaim, 'those who take my advice will be fine and dry while you others....well, I've no sympathy for you!' "You know",* continued Miss Carter, *"the number of people who bought from him was incredible; every time he came on I was amazed."* The van, according to Miss Carter had one side which was lowered giving a platform from which the 'Umbrella Man' would go through his routine, those on looking, could see behind him in the interior of the van all his stock, each in their respective pigeon holes. Like most of the auctioneering type of tradesman this umbrella man had an associate within the crowd. Miss Carter: *"upon making a sale the umbrella would be thrown towards his helper, who'd collect the money enabling his partner's sales talk to continue, any change would be handed over as quickly as possible with no break from this routine."* As previously stated the black pudding stalls had always enjoyed a good trade and they were at this time still as popular as ever, as too were the ice cream stalls. By now there were about five or six ice cream vendors on the market with the most popular ones being Talco's and Siddall's. Talco's ice cream business was now being run by Joe Talco son of the founder John, and besides being on the market ground Talco's ice cream carts, like many others, could also be seen at many sites around the borough. Working for Joe Talco during the 1930s was a young lady named Esther Adams Lee, who today recalls; *"I worked seven days a week for Joe, obviously not always on the market, for which I received 5s a day plus food and overalls. To me Talco's ice cream was lovely, it was made in their own premises near to Charlestown station and I'm sure he made it with best butter, one of the first to do so. "We sold our cornets at a halfpenny; 1d and 2d, children and adults alike just loved them especially with a good splash of raspberry. Another constant customer who enjoyed a regular 1d cornet actually frightened me, Jock was his name and he would stick his head into the cart and refuse to move until he'd had his ice cream."* Jock was a giant grey carthorse that belonged to Joe Talco. *"I remember during the wakes week that I had to work much longer hours on the market ground, often until the pubs had closed, it was then the last bus home."*

During the research for this book, we have had the pleasure of meeting and talking with a great number of market traders and indeed with many members of the public, they being the shoppers who over the years have visited the market in their thousands. Upon interviewing those with recollections prior to 1950 we discovered that one trader's name in particular came to everyone's lips. Even the people whose own personal memories were drawn from more modern times still knew his name, having learned of him from other ex-traders or older members of the family, all of them spoke with a great affection. So who is this person who everyone describes in such glowing terms? The man is Harry Gilbert, whose name was synonymous with watches on Ashton's market ground for so many years. Harry, along with his two brothers Charles and Mick were the sons of Barnet Gilbert, who in 1868 founded a precious metals business. It was Charles who first stood on Ashton's market ground and he too was a wholesaler and retailer in jewellery and also acted as a pawnbroker. With very little money about during the period between the Boer War and the First World War, he as a pawnbroker amassed a great deal of stock and the only places he could off-load the forfeits and unredeemed pledges were on the markets of the north west. Charles successfully stood various markets including Ashton, Denton, Hyde, Oldham, Farnworth and many more. Finding it difficult even with help, to appear at all these markets, Charles gave his stalls at Dukinfield and Blackburn to Mick, while Harry took on Ashton, Denton and Hyde. It was a great belief of the Gilbert family that they needn't be bible thumpers or have to attend church to be a good person, for to them just making someone happy or doing a kindness was itself carrying out God's work. If anyone needed help, no matter what there station in life, they would freely give it never wanting any praise, reward or publicity. Like his brothers, Harry thought that a 'good name' was worth more than money. It was never widely known that Harry Gilbert subscribed to many local charities and that he was responsible for many of Ashton's old aged pensioners receiving a weekly allowance, for which he expected nothing in return. From his stall positioned near to the town hall, Harry would draw huge crowds, often so big that they encroached on the area fronting the neighbouring stalls stopping those traders from doing any business. However, this never seemed to worry them, for they knew when Harry's crowd had finally dispersed he would always join them to help with the selling of their goods. Everyone who has spoken of Harry described him as being one of the most respected and fairest of people they had ever come across, he was said to have been the most genuine trader there was, a real honest man. On his market days Harry, resplendent looking with his clipped military style moustache and sporting a bowler hat, would open up the back of a pocket watch showing everyone the movements, should you find that these watches ever go wrong, I'll change them for you, he would say. It is said that there was a time when everyone in Ashton owned a Harry Gilbert watch and not many if any were returned. Although having a warehouse in Manchester from where he conducted his business, Harry's first love was the market.

Harry Gilbert in his retirement years and still looking the dapper gentleman.

Sam Bates was another whose name was long associated with the market for many years and was perhaps better known to the general public as

'Sam the pot man'. Before venturing out as a trader in his own right Sam had learned the business working for Gibson's china shop on Warrington Street, later building up a successful warehouse along with his many market stalls, of which Ashton proved the most lucrative. Sam was a real showman and the crowds gathered in their numbers to watch him pitching his wares at his stall under the market clock. They would stand open mouthed; mesmerised as he balanced a full dinner service or tea set under one arm, before throwing it up in the air and catching it again, waiting in vain for the day they would see him drop and smash one. Sam was eventually joined by his nephew Arthur Marsh, who later became a member of Ashton council. Between them the pair at their Cotton Street warehouse would sort out tea-chests full of crockery, which came direct from the Potteries, they would then spend time making them up into sets ready for sale on the market. In those days the stallholder not only had to be a salesman but also a comedian and entertainer, for after attracting a crowd there was an art in keeping them. If a crowd was indifferent or apathetic Sam would have no hesitation in telling them all to go away, for he knew he could soon attract more. Once he had them in a good mood, he would start his patter, a familiar routine performed by them is recalled by Sam's son-in-law Mr Underwood, who for a time also worked with them; *"If a crowd was a bit dull or awkward then we had to get them going, one routine was for me to bring out from under the stall a large chamber pot, which I waved about for all to see. Sam would stand back aghast, feigning shock and would cry, hey hang on you can't bring that out here. Which resulted in a lot of laughter, my reply was to say, but this woman here asked me if we had a large white tea-cup, which usually brought about even more laughter, it didn't matter if we sold the chamber pot or not, it was just a matter of putting them in the right mood...and ready for Sam or Arthur's sales talk. "It was no use bringing out the dearer stuff right away, so they would start with things like saucers at a halfpenny each. Lines such as the good tea sets which sold for around 2s 6d would follow later, after which it would be back to the cheaper items".* With no market on Tuesday, Sam would use the time going around to most of the local public houses taking their orders for new glasses. Incidentally, these glasses would have been taken to the weights and measures department at the town hall prior to their delivery to the publicans, where they were tested and officially stamped. In later years Sam and Arthur also established a stall inside the market hall.

HOTELS, CLUBS, and all in the CATERING TRADE
RENEW YOUR STOCKS of CROCKERY at——

BATES & MARSH'S **MARKET HALL, ASHTON-U-LYNE**

Available from stock: CUPS and SAUCERS, Rolled-edge PLATES in 5-, 6-, 7-, and 8-inch sizes. May we quote you ?

Besides the event of the annual wakes fair there were also other times when the market ground was cleared of stalls. One such time was Whit Friday to allow the local churches to assemble for a service prior to setting off in procession around the town. In the morning the congregation of the United Churches would gather, followed around lunch time by the Catholic churches. The Church of England always held their services at the Parish church before proceeding with their walk of witness sometime in the afternoon. Under the market clock tower a platform was erected from where the services were conducted and from where the brass bands played to accompany the hymn singing. Later in the day these brass bands along with others would return to the ground to compete in the annual brass band contest. Huge crowds would gather during the evening to watch and listen to the bands competing against each other, which of course brought their day to a pleasant end. The judges for this contest would gather together in the market office in the clock tower, from where they could hear the music but were unaware which band was actually playing.

The Whit Walk procession passing the Market Hall at the junction of Wellington Road and Market Street. The Queen's Picture House is in the background which today is Wetherspoon's 'Ash Tree' Public House.

Since opening in 1882 the fish market had brought about many complaints, the majority coming from the general public who often voiced their opinions in the local press and in many a conversation. From its early days the main complaint had been regarding the smell and throughout the years this always remained as the major problem. It is claimed that cleanliness was never what one would expect in such a place and although there were always some form of hygiene regulations, though not as stringent as today's, they were hardly ever adhered to. One would not need to be inside the fish market to be overcome by its stench, for even pedestrians outside would often hurry past in order to avoid the lingering odour. Little if anything had been done to improve this section of the market and for over 50 years the original glazed brick walls remained, as too did the central drain on the floor which never received its proper hosing down. Killed off by its own smell the fish market was finally closed down in 1935, and this part of the building was now to undergo considerable reconstruction at a cost of around £5,000 before reopening as the new electricity showrooms.

Amusements have always been a regular feature of Ashton's market ground, with some form of ride or sideshow continually being sited at the Warrington Street end of the market, not just at wakes time but throughout the year. Leonard Corns recalls some of the many attractions that visited the market in the years prior to the outbreak of World War II; *"Mander's used to come on with lions in an animal show but not the kind of show that appeared in years gone-by. There was also the 'Wall of Death' or the perpendicular wall, I remember once they asked if anyone wanted to bring their own motor bike and have a go. "The usual riders on the wall of death always used light machines, unlike the huge heavy one brought along by one young eager volunteer. Undaunted, he sat astride his machine as the door was slammed shut behind him; he revved up his bike and set off to a loud chorus of cheers. These cheers soon turned to laughter however, as while still riding around the slope before tackling the actual wall, he fell off his bike, a result of dizziness. He wasn't at all amused as the crowds laughed and jeered. "I can also remember watching one show on the wall of death when a rider went around with a sidecar, and sat in this sidecar was a fully grown lion. I remember thinking at the time that this wasn't a nice thing for this poor animal, to be driven around in circles. It's nice to know that such a thing wouldn't be allowed today. "A regular visitor on a mid-week day was an escapologist who put on a straight jacket and asked members of the public to tie him up. As they usually do, within a few minutes of wriggling about he had escaped and was out among the crowd taking a collection".* In addition to the August wakes fair, there was a period when a smaller Easter fair would also assemble. Opening on the market ground on the Thursday prior to Easter and then on the Saturday and Monday. This well patronised fair combined a number of small stalls, notably the roll-a-penny, coconut shies and other games of chance along with a few rides, usually Hibbert's Jumping Horses and Steam Yachts.

A lion on the wall of death was not such an uncommon sight in the 1920s and 30s.

With the outbreak of the Second World War many stallholders were called up to serve in the forces. Ashton council gave all traders the assurance that at war's end they would be allowed to return to the market and take up their stalls once again. The market itself suffered so much at this time that not only were there a number of boarded up stalls in the market hall but many of the outside stall holders had ceased business, certainly in appearance it was now looking rather run down. With so many foodstuffs available only on ration, shopping during the war years could not have been an easy task. The Butchers and confectionery businesses bore the brunt of the war-time ration queues yet it was at this time that Robert Gleave opened his confectionery stall inside the market hall. The business is still trading successfully today (2009) being run by Robert's son Barry Gleave.

TENDER FORM.

To Mr. ~~Jesse Lowe~~ SIDNEY SCRAGG,
Market Superintendent.

I am willing to take the Stall No. 6 in the Market Hall, Ashton-under-Lyne, and to pay therefor a Rental of £ 1 : 12 : 6 per week. And I undertake to occupy the said Stall as tenant of the Corporation for a period of not less than twelve weeks, and not to sublet the same.

Signed R. Gleave
Address 97 Marlborough St
Ashton U Lyne

Date 7th March 1940

State Nature of Business (Bought Confectionery)

Tender form signed by Robert Gleave in 1940 stating that he was willing to pay £1.12s.6d per week for a stall in the indoor market for the retail of 'Bought in' Confectionary'.

One commodity which remained readily available off ration was tripe, which enabled such stalls including those belonging to Entwistle's and the U.C.P to continue with a steady trade. Entwistle's had traded inside the market since 1867. The original business had been founded by Richard Entwistle from a shop on Wellington Road. Living on the premises Richard was able to use the cellar for much of the preparation work, but it wasn't long before a more suitable cold store and works was obtained on Conduit Street near to the River Tame. After Richard retired the business was taken over by his son Alfred and then in turn by his son, who was also named Richard. It was the latter who was responsible for a new factory being built which was considered to be one of the area's best. Through the generations the business grew and besides running their own shops and stalls they supplied many other businesses as well. Richard continued with the tradition of naming boys in the family Richard and Alfred and it is the latter who reveals; *"as a child my job was to get all the copper*

TRIPE: Tripe and cow-heels are already perfectly cooked. Instead of burning black diamonds in hours of cooking you can serve tripe and cow-heels hot in a few minutes. Fuel, work and time saved. Tripe [illegible]d. per lb.; cow-heels 4d. per lb.

An early advertisement for Entwistle's Tripe.

coins together and rub salt all over them. Selling tripe was a continually wet job and if the coins were not salted it caused verdigris which would turn all of them green and that meant the banks wouldn't accept them. "I enjoyed working on the stall and to do the serving I had to stand on a box, customers always seemed to want to be served by the same person every time they came. I remember some wanted me to serve them all the time while others preferred mother, and some father. "One funny incident I recall happened one Saturday afternoon probably around 2pm. It was at this time when the market hall had quietened down a little, that the opportunity arose for the stallholders to have their dinners. Now Marjorie, my sister, who was looking after one of our stalls, took up this chance, as did Mrs Dewhurst who was working on the adjoining U.C.P. stall. "Finnerty's cafe sold their famous potato pie in portions priced at 3d and 4d with the costliest portion being larger and served with crust. Mrs Dewhurst this day purchased the bigger helping, complete with crust, while Marjorie not being a big eater didn't have so much. The combination of the hot summer day along with that of a full stomach soon had its after-effects on Mrs Dewhurst, who began to feel rather tired. She decided to sit down for a while which proved to be a very costly move on her part, for she soon fell asleep. Marjorie took full advantage of this situation by letting her sleep and consequently took all her business". Finnerty's cafe at the outbreak of the war was being run by Mrs Florrie Finnerty, daughter-in-law of Susanna Finnerty, who had taken over after the death of her husband John. The Finnerty family had made this market cafe a traditional place renowned for its home cooked roast pork and ham and of course the legendary potato pie. With the rationing of certain foodstuffs throughout, and even after the war, it became very difficult for restaurant and cafe owners to run their businesses. Official permits were required before they could obtain any of the rationed or controlled goods and consequently were restricted in what they could obtain to serve to the public. Throughout these very difficult years Florrie Finnerty still managed to keep the market cafe open and maintained a cheery meeting place for all. Mr Albert Braithwaite aged 64 recalls paying regular Saturday morning visits to Finnerty's cafe as a 12 year old boy during the war; *"My mother would always send me to the market hall on Saturday for her newspaper. She could only afford one paper a week and it was nearly always Saturdays that she would get. I was always one of the first at the newsagents in the market, the one situated against the wall on the Market Street end of the building. After buying the paper I would wander through the hall in the direction of the market ground. Now, mother didn't like me reading the paper so I would call into Finnerty's to buy myself a drink and have a quick flick through its pages. I don't think my mum ever found out about this, even though the paper was always a little crumpled when she got it. If she had not been so busy seeing to my younger brother I'm sure she would have realised just how long I'd been away. "That same newsagents is still in the market today* (1993) *and has been there for as long as I can remember."* At the time recalled by Mr Braithwaite the newsagent's was being run by Mr Frank

Hindle. Frank had taken over the business from his parents in 1932 for whom he had been working since a boy of 12 in 1898. The stall continued to be run by the Hindle family up until 1999.

Please quote Ministry Reference in reply.

MINISTRY OF FOOD

Telephone: Ashton 1625

Your Reference ....

M.O.F. Reference ....LW/EO....

NATIONAL REGISTRATION

ASHTON-UNDER-LYNE FOOD OFFICE

N.W.2. NTG

99, WARRINGTON STREET.

ASHTON-UNDER-LYNE, LANCS.

26th September, 1949.

Dear Madam,

Your application for a duplicate licence and the extension of your catering licence in respect of the premises Market Restaurant, 43, Market Hall, Ashton-u-Lyne has been granted and I enclose herewith licence number EL/NW2/22.

You will also be granted permits to obtain the following rationed and controlled foods -

Bacon and Ham uncooked, Biscuits rusks and crispbreads, Bread, Butter, Cakes, Coffee, Eggs, Fruit bottled or canned, Jam and marmalade, Lard and compound Lard, Meat canned or preserved (other than canned corned beef, canned corned pork and canned corned mutton), Milk fresh, Mincemeat, Rabbits, Rice and edible rice products, Sugar, Tea, and Vegetables dried.

Yours faithfully,

L. Butlin,
F.E.O. and N.R.O.

Mrs. Waters
43, Market Hall,
Ashton-u-Lyne.

An official letter from The Ministry of Food to 'Finnerty's Café' – Explaining that permits would be granted enabling rationed & controlled foods to be obtained.

In keeping with other public buildings throughout the town, fire watchers were appointed during the war, to carry out duties within the market hall. Stirrup pumps, hatchets, steel helmets, buckets and long handled scoops were among the items of equipment purchased by the market committee for use by the traders. A number of air-raid shelters were situated in nearby streets, but aware that a great many people may be at the market during a raid, the tenants approached the council to ask for the erection of additional shelters nearer to the market. One such shelter which was provided was situated at the bottom of the market ground, near to the Reporter office. After the war this shelter was utilised by the market for other purposes. The open space of the market ground and the many stalls boarded up inside the hall, proved an attraction for the children and many spent happy hours playing and running around much to the annoyance of the public and remaining stall-holders. One person who remembered undertaking such antics as a child was John Latus, later to become a market trader himself following in his father's footsteps. When aged about 10 years, and at a time when he was joining in the fun playing tick with other youngsters, John also became friendly with a Mrs Johnson, a trader who sold second hand clothing. John was soon keeping out of trouble as his time was now occupied working for this elderly lady. Mrs Johnson kept her stock of clothes in large wicker skips, and it was John's job to push these to and from the market. Working Monday and Friday, before and after school, and also on Saturday, John received a sum of 2s 6d for his endeavours. At this time there would have been no more than three rows of stalls situated directly in front of the market building. The rest of the market ground between these stalls and Warrington Street was vacant space. It was in this area that Mrs Johnson would join several other traders who all sold their goods from tarpaulin sheets on the ground.

During 1945 just prior to the end of the war, both the market hall and market ground came in for some severe criticism from a number of town councillors, traders and general public. Leading the attack on the indoor market was Alderman E. Meeks who referred to the hall as being smelly and dirty; while Councillor J. Howarth spoke out on behalf of many residents regarding their growing concerns relating to fairground caravans on the market ground. Alderman Meeks informed the February meeting of the council that people walking through the hall had been disgusted by what they had seen and that anyone who said that it was clean must be blind. Wartime pressures had meant the upkeep of any public building had been almost impossible to maintain, as both materials and manpower were simply unavailable. Consequently buildings soon became neglected and Ashton market hall was no exception. Under those circumstances Alderman Meeks' attack may at first have seemed uncalled for, however he did draw attention to some conditions to which the war could not be used as an excuse. A smell of cats in various parts of the building appalled Alderman Meeks, so much so, that on one occasion he personally brought it to the attention of the market superintendent. As one would expect, in the face of such criticism the market committee chairman, Councillor E. Clarke denied that the hall was smelly, apart from the smells usually associated with a provisions shop. Councillor J. W. Whitworth himself a former chairman of the market committee fully agreed with councillor Clarke, but admitted however, that the hall had become unsightly due to the fact that no decorating had been done, but provision had been made for it to be carried out as soon as the opportunity arose. Both councillors resented the statement that the hall smelled, claiming that it was cleaned properly and regularly by attendants. A letter which appeared in the local paper from a Mr Mitchell of Clayton Bridge and a former Ashton resident did seem to confirm that the cleaning of the hall left something to be desired, he wrote of...seeing heaps of refuge and decaying vegetables combining to create a disagreeable atmosphere. Though not wanting to be too critical in war time Mr Mitchell added... even in war time, soap and water was readily available, is it only reasonable for premises so largely devoted to the sale of foodstuffs to have clean floors. Perhaps then the claims of Alderman Meeks did have some foundation; after all they did prompt Mr Hartley, president of the market tenants association, to air the views of the traders. Mr Hartley called the market hall outdated with its flag flooring, it was badly heated, so much so that during one cold spell the temperature was 42 degrees with the floor being covered in wet mud. He continued by saying that there was poor lighting and many of the stalls were unsuited for the class of trade for which they were used, in all he thought a more up to date building was required. As to the smells, Mr Hartley confirmed the statements of councillors Clarke and Whitworth saying that they were produced by having the various trades grouped together, accidentally and not planned and that indeed they were not too unpleasant; though he did admit that the covers around many of the empty stalls did smell and should be removed.

TRY F. OLDFIELD'S EXCELLENT CAKES

Cherry, Madeiras, Sultana, Cocoanut,
Rice, Currant, and Seed Loaves

HIGHEST QUALITY INGREDIENTS USED!

Only 6d. each. Can be obtained at—

Oldfield's Stall, Market Hall, Ashton

also sold at 320 Shops in Ashton and Surrounding Districts

Further criticism of the market around this time was brought about by the number of fairground caravans which had become a permanent fixture in the market area. Around the end of September each year it was standard practice for the country's travelling showpeople to return to their respective home towns where they would remain until the following spring. So, it was quite normal for caravans belonging to the local showpeople to be seen parked on the market during the winter months. However due to the outbreak of War in September 1939 and the many restrictions imposed they were now unable to move on as usual. Consequently their caravans had essentially created a shanty town and the conditions in which they were living did nothing to enhance the shopping area. Councillor J. Howarth was quoted at the time as saying, *"even if we look at the market ground through the most rosy of coloured glasses we cannot say that it is anything but an eyesore. "The town hall being the civic centre lost much of its dignity with such contraptions being in such close proximity and the situation must be a nightmare for residents in the immediate vicinity. "One only had to cross the market ground after dark to realise the moral hazards of the conglomeration of fairground equipment".* Yes there were caravans and indeed a mini fairground featuring such rides as Inglewood's Noah's Ark, Arthur Macey's Dodgems, Shaw's Moon Rocket along with the ever popular Waltzer and numerous side stalls. Even so, perhaps under the circumstances councillor Howarth's remarks were unfair as the showpeople inhabiting the caravans and running the fair were the children, womenfolk and the elderly – most of the able bodied showmen had either volunteered or had been called up for national service. Taking everything in to consideration it would seem that shopping at this time would not have been a pleasant task. In April of the year, with the markets still coming in for criticism, Councillor Allan requested that tolerance and patience be showed towards the fairground people, they were because of the situation, unable to move on, but once the war was over they would once again be mobile. Later in the month it was revealed that the market hall would indeed be decorated, in colours of cream, blue and light green, which was good news to many. Later Councillor E. Clarke said, *"Every effort had been made by the committee and as an increase of lighting would soon be allowed, it was intended to make the market hall into one of the finest shopping centres in the north of England".* However, regarding the caravans on the open market Councillor Clarke's commented, *"As there is no evidence of any danger to health and as their removal would have resulted in a loss to the council of £300 per annum, the council felt they could not recommend they be moved".*

Replica of the Old Cross - Today only the top section remains.

In the first chapter of this book we told of how in 1829 the old market cross was taken down and removed to Stamford Park and of a replica standing in St. Michael's Square. This replica was unveiled by Alderman J. Q. Massey on Saturday October 27th 1945. In attendance for the occasion was the Mayor, Alderman W. H. Flowers and Canon H. Whewell the rector of Ashton, along with several other dignitaries. Although the weather was quite unpleasant with rain falling, a good-sized crowd had nonetheless gathered to witness the proceedings. After pulling a string to release the Union Flag which had covered the cross Alderman Massey said, *"I unveil this replica of the old cross in the hope that the younger generation will take it as a token of Christianity in this part of the country".* He went on to recite a self-written poem from which the following is taken. *'Here farm producers weekly came, to trade the fruits of toil and earth, and thrifty housewives strove in vein, to under-rate the yeoman's worth'.* Initially it had been hoped to re-erect the old cross but it was thought, due to its age, that the removal from Stamford Park may have caused it irreparable damage. However, even this replica has over the years gone through change, with only the top section surviving today.

Two years after the initial outcry over the encampment of the showpeople on the market ground, renewed pressure was being put on the council, whom many thought were ignoring the situation due to the rents they were receiving. Reflecting the views of the public a reporter in the local paper wrote... *"the present motley assortment of caravans and coconut shies maintained for the benefit of the irresponsible element should be cleared away to some vacant and less conspicuous spot where rent could still be charged, it is about time the centre of town was invested with a little dignity".* Shortly after this latest outcry the council made public their intentions of finally moving on all the fairground people. Incidentally the annual wakes fair continued to be a regular event on the market ground for the next thirteen years, until town centre redevelopment brought an end to this tradition.

In 1947 a name long associated with the market ceased to trade, that of Richard Entwistle tripe dressers. The business being sold to Dixon's Pork butchers by the founder's grandson. Alfred Entwistle whose father made the sale remembers; *"I don't know why he sold out, it came as a complete surprise, maybe it was because tripe was slowly going out of favour. I had suggested that we brought in other things like cooked meats but dad wouldn't have it". "I'm sure if we had done it, their sales would have eventually overtaken tripe and he might not then have sold. "Dad was too independent for his own good, at one time Septimus Hill founder of U.C.P. asked him to join him, it was at the formation of U.C.P but dad said no. Years later he was asked again when U.C.P was a success, but once more he said no. My brother and I continued to work for the new owners for some time".* The sale of Entwistle's business to Dixon's also included their factory on Conduit Street adjacent to the River Tame. A year later and another butchery business was involved in a takeover. This however, was under different circumstances as the proprietor of Whittam's Butchers had sadly been killed in action during the war. Rather than continue with the business herself Mrs Whittam decided to sell to David Conn one of her employees. With the exception of the time he served in the Middle East during World War II David had worked for the Whittam's from the age of fifteen. From acquiring the business in 1948 he built up a good relationship with his customers and during the oncoming years became a well respected member of the market community. David was still trading at the age of 87 having completed 72 years in the market hall when the tragic fire of 2004 occurred.

For a considerable number of years members of the Seldon family had been hiring out stalls for use on Ashton market and at one time also managed those belonging to the council. In 1947 this practice was being continued by brothers John and James Seldon, whose business, like others had suffered somewhat during the war years. However, in 1947 their plight worsened when the council decided to erect and take control of renting all stalls – effectively bringing an end to the Seldon's business locally. These council owned stalls brought to the market ground for the first time electric lighting which had cost them £1,700 to install. Having introduced the new stalls the council subsequently increased rents - a 12ft stall was 12s and an 8ft stall 10s. Both these rents included a daily, all the year round charge for the lighting, which in the case of a 12ft stall was 1s 2d. After discussing the new rents amongst themselves and agreeing that the council was asking too much, the traders decided to protest by boycotting the Monday market day. Arrangements were made for their first action to be taken on Monday January 6th 1947 when they hoped that all traders, with the exception of those selling food, would play a part. Pickets were out early on the bitterly cold Monday morning but were not called into any action as only one trader, a permitted food retailer, had turned up. Because, in their opinion the boycott had been successful, and the fact that a mid-week council meeting had been held without the issue being discussed, the traders continued their boycott on the following Friday, Saturday and once again on Monday. A meeting was held to try and resolve the matter on January 13th, but both sides failed to reach any agreement. The council pointed out that the rent they were asking was a reasonable one in view of the installation costs. The traders however, were incensed that they were being asked to pay a daily all year round charge for lighting, which in the summertime was not required. Later in the week, the traders took a different direction in order to win their case. They agreed to resume trading from Friday paying the tolls requested, but as one trader put it: *"under protest and without prejudice,"* While trading under these circumstances they were now looking into the possibility of taking the council to court. The traders' secretary had delved into the local bye-laws and he suspected that the council could not impose the extra charge. The passing of time however, saw no further action of any nature being taken by the traders, suggesting that they must have known they could not pursue the matter to their satisfaction.

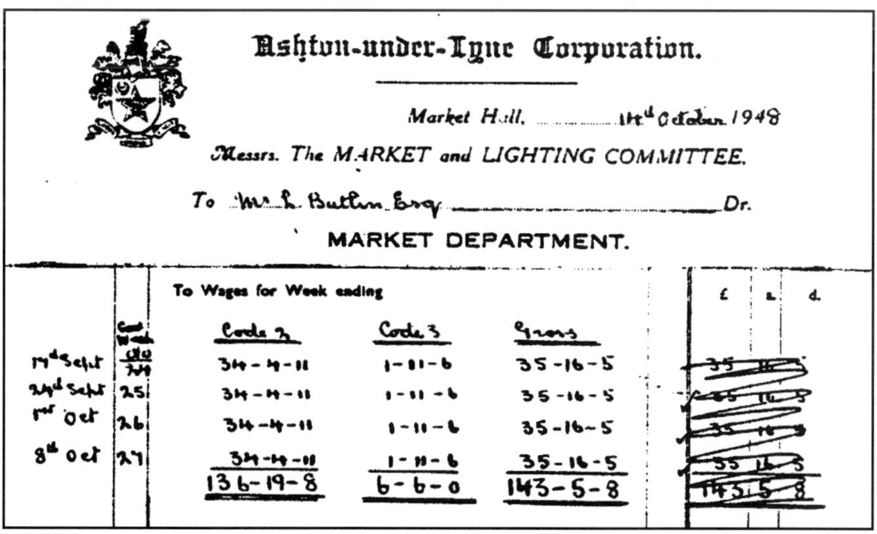

Ashton-under-Lyne Corporation.

Market Hall, 14th October 1948

Messrs. The MARKET and LIGHTING COMMITTEE.

To Mr L. Butler Esq Dr.

MARKET DEPARTMENT.

To Wages for Week ending

	Cont. Week	Code 2	Code 3	Gross	£ s. d.
17th Sept	24	34-4-11	1-11-6	35-16-5	35 16 5
24th Sept	25	34-4-11	1-11-6	35-16-5	35 16 5
1st Oct	26	34-4-11	1-11-6	35-16-5	35 16 5
8th Oct	27	34-4-11	1-11-6	35-16-5	35 16 5
		136-19-8	6-6-0	143-5-8	143 5 8

Market wage bill for a four week period during 1948 amounted to £143 5s 8d

A rather austere looking market (1946/47)

Another problem brought about by the council's ownership of stalls, was one of storage, for at this time the stalls were still removed at the end of each trading day. Previously when Seldon's had managed the stalls, they had the benefit of their own nearby storage yard, but the council were not so lucky. The particularly bad winter of 1947 also caused damage to several of the new stalls making the matter of their storage all the more necessary. However, as urgent as it may have been it was to be June before it was reported that a shelter was ready and that it was just a matter of awaiting the arrival of trolleys to help with the transportation. Eventually the old air-raid shelter which stood at the end of the market ground was given over for storage of the stalls. Past market superintendent Philip Poulter recalls; *"they were stacked in the shelter....and what couldn't go inside were put on top of the concrete roof. In time more and more had to be stacked up around the shelter and odd ones even had to be put at the rear of the town hall".*

Having seen his business partnership with his brother come to an end, John Seldon seeking a new venture bought a kiddies roundabout positioning it next to the existing ride owned by Billy Cooke. Although a travelling showman Billy Cooke had been established on the market with his ride for many years and also owned a similar roundabout at Hyde market. Competition between Billy and newcomer John Seldon never really materialised as Billy thought there was not enough trade to warrant two roundabouts. However, another local family of show-people, the Rust's believed Billy was wrong. Consequently, Nora Rust spoke with market superintendent Sidney Scragg about taking over Billy's site. As Billy still had his roundabout at Hyde to run and knowing if necessary that he could still go on the road, he agreed to Nora Rust's proposition. Billy's departure from Ashton market was the end of an era, for he had been a permanent fixture there for more years than people could remember. Throughout his time on the market Billy had in his employment a certain Mr Harrison. This happy bowler-hatted character known by many as 'Roundabout Charlie' was said to have been a little slow-thinking. Consequently, while Billy collected the pennies from the children 'Charlie' had the simple task of turning the handle to keep the ride going around. During the period when rides and amusements would remain open late on Saturday nights, Billy's roundabout was one of the few which closed early – by 6pm Billy was on a tram journeying home. Within the space of half an hour 'Roundabout Charlie' was back and within no time the covers were off and the ride going around. The difference now being that he was collecting and keeping all the money. Not bad for someone supposedly slow-thinking - it seemed as though everyone apart from Billy knew just what was going on. Not long after Nora Rust had taken over Billy's site, John Seldon's brother James erected a third roundabout adding to the competition. In time both James Seldon and the Rust's introduced children's swings onto the market. Before her marriage into the Rust family Nora had been a Mulhearn a well established family of show-people who travelled with their fairground attractions. The Rust family however, had their roots firmly set in Ashton and for generations had been associated with the market providing skips and oil lamps to traders. Shortly after her marriage Nora introduced her husband to life on the road, but when children came onto the scene this lifestyle was to change. Nora was never keen on living in caravans and eventually bought a house on Katherine Street. Her husband continued to move around with various rides but Nora became more or less permanently at home with their children. The opportunity to establish a roundabout on the market ground was she believed one not to be missed. The passing of time showed Nora had good judgement as the ride remained within the family for many years eventually passing to her son Fred.

Some time after the electric lighting had been introduced to the market ground the Rust family had an idea how they could make a little extra income. Ashton's main market days were Monday, Friday and Saturday which saw the traders utilising the electricity provided by the council. However, on Tuesday, Wednesday and Thursday when many of the greengrocers stalls were still open for business electricity was not available. Within the cellar of the Rust family home were stored a good many oil lamps which in years gone-by had been hired out to traders – this seemed a good point at which to reintroduce them to the market. The lamps would be distributed around dinner time and collected around 7pm after the mill workers had made their way home and the traders had finished their day. Eventually the Rusts were given permission by the council to generate their own power to light and operate all three roundabouts. The Rust's used an old double-decker bus to store the lighting and to house a good sized generator to make life easier on the roundabouts – no more turning the handle to make the ride go around. Once consent had been received from the council the Rust's also began to provide enough power to light the greengrocers stalls (on non-market days) thus doing away with the old oil lamps. The stall holders were charge per bulb so the more bulbs they used the more money was made.

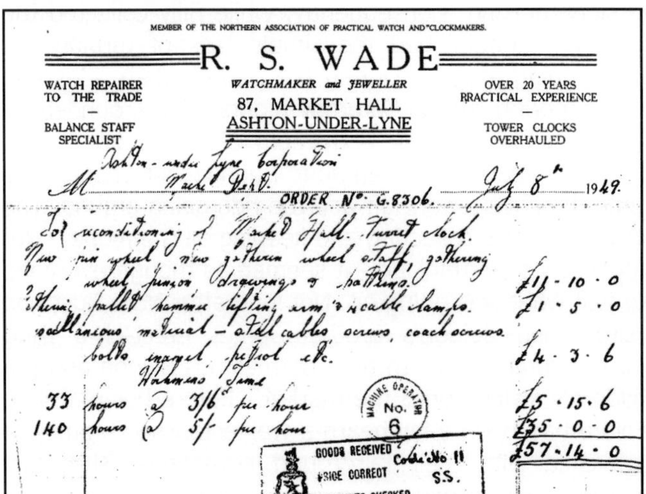
MEMBER OF THE NORTHERN ASSOCIATION OF PRACTICAL WATCH AND CLOCKMAKERS.

R. S. WADE

WATCH REPAIRER TO THE TRADE — BALANCE STAFF SPECIALIST

WATCHMAKER and JEWELLER
87, MARKET HALL
ASHTON-UNDER-LYNE

OVER 20 YEARS PRACTICAL EXPERIENCE — TOWER CLOCKS OVERHAULED

M Ashton-under-Lyne Corporation, Market Dept. ORDER No. G.8306. July 8th 1949.

To reconditioning of Market Hall Turret clock.

	£11 · 10 · 0
	£1 · 5 · 0
	£4 · 3 · 6
33 hours @ 3/6 per hour	£5 · 15 · 6
140 hours @ 5/- per hour	£35 · 0 · 0
	£57 · 14 · 0

MACHINE OPERATOR No. 6

GOODS RECEIVED — PRICE CORRECT — ACCOUNTS CHECKED

Market Hall tenant R. S. Wade, Watchmaker charged the council £57.14s for repairs to the market hall clock in 1948.

Chapter Four.

To market, to market a gallop a trot,
to buy some meat to put in the pot;
Threepence a quarter, a groat a side,
if it hadn't been killed it must have died.

The Market Ground in the 1950s viewed from Bow Street

Motor vehicles were still very hard to obtain in post-war Britain, for there had been no commercial production during the war years, and indeed petrol itself was still a rare commodity. Both these facts combined to make life very difficult for anyone attempting to start their own market business. It was a direct consequence of this fact that John Latus Snr decided to purchase a pony and cart which would give him the transport he needed for his fledgling greengrocery business. His working day would start at around 4am with the feeding of the pony, before setting off on the journey to Manchester's Smithfield market for his stock. With imported produce still being unavailable, it was just a matter of obtaining home-grown produce only. Unlike today where there are many varieties of fruits and vegetables available all year round, at this time availability depended solely on the season of the year. For a time, especially during the particularly bad winter of 1947, there was hardly anything around, as most of the potatoes and winter vegetables had been frozen in the ground, which gave the life of a greengrocer an added burden. Mr Latus' son John Latus Jnr recalls: *"Even when faced with some early difficulties my dad managed to build up a successful business and eventually the pony was replaced by an old Ford, then later by a bigger lorry. "We lived in a cottage house on Tatton Street which was one of the many heavily populated streets near to the market. Most people who lived there either worked in the mines or the cotton mills, so we didn't need an alarm clock, because about 6am we'd hear the sound of all the clogs clattering over the cobbled stones as the people made their way to work. Those who worked in the mills would pass the market on their way back home, so my dad used to trade after 5.30pm waiting for the mill girls, who provided us with at least an extra half-hour of business".*

At the start of the 1950s most forms of rationing were still in existence, but with the re-emergence of the market gardens on Ashton Moss the town's market began to return to something like its former self. The market gardens made all the difference to the outside market providing as they did plenty of local produce for the now ever increasing fruit and vegetable stalls. It has been said that at one point during the 1950s there were at least thirty-seven greengrocers and salad merchants trading. There was now a huge amount of food coming onto Ashton market, Robinson Brothers alone had three 20ft lorries unloading greengrocery for their stalls.

One of the many greengrocers was John Kelly (pictured)
The business today is still with the same family

Among the many new fruit and vegetable traders established in the early 1950s was Les Crossland. Like most newcomers to the market Les had started as a pitcher, this was the term given to a trader who brought his own stall which he erected each day. Les actually used two old doors placed upon trestles for his pitch. Most of the pitchers were allocated space near to the roundabouts from where over time they would eventually be offered one of the stalls belonging to the market. Derek Duckworth a ten year old schoolboy at the time was offered a job as a tea boy with Les

Crossland, and recalled, *"When Les was eventually offered a stall it was on the edge of the market ground on Katherine Street facing the Town Hall, "For fruit and veg this was a bad area as all the other greengrocers were on the other side of the market on Bow Street. "In time however, he did manage a move to Bow Street after he had gone into partnership with Alfred Bardsley".* Alfred Bardsley had a warehouse at the rear of the Friendship public house on Old Street in which he stored his produce and from where he would replenish his stall on a daily basis. Those traders without such premises would simply throw a cover over their stock and tie it to their stall where it remained until the next trading day.

There were also stalls selling a variety of other foodstuffs including bread, eggs, meat, chickens, bacon etc. Although the full market was only operating on three days, the greengrocery stalls opened for business six days a week. On the non-market days these greengrocers mainly traded on passing custom created by the close proximity of the trolley buses, which started and ended their journeys on Bow Street. *"I can remember trolleybuses actually bumping into some stalls"*, said John Latus; *"It was at wakes time when the market had been cleared of the stalls, to accommodate the fair. Some traders were fortunate in being allowed to carry on with their business from stalls erected on Market Street and Bow Street. The buses would often bump into the stalls situated near to the corner of Bow Street as it was so congested. "For us it was the busiest time of year, because half the greengrocers couldn't get a pitch on the streets, there just wasn't the room. As my dad was one of the first to be established after the war, they gave him a premier pitch at the top of the Market Avenue. We used to take more money that week than we did at any other time of year".*

Still pulling in the crowds. 1950s wakes fair

Happily for the local children the ice-cream vendors had soon returned to the market ground at the war's end. Initially they used small trailers, with somewhat cramped space for the sales assistant. However, the 1950's saw the introduction of new trailers that were much larger than their immediate post-war counterparts. The new Siddall's trailer was distinctive with its colours of maroon and cream. The cream coloured trailer of Howard's featured cowboy pictorials, very appealing to the kiddies. Beryl Dawson, now Mrs. Beryl Grimes worked as a young girl during the 1950s for Howard's and recalled; *"I was about fourteen when I worked for them. I would be in the market trailer all day on Saturdays, I didn't mind as all the*

'The small post-war ice cream trailers..........

..........and their new replacements'

young lads would come and 'chat us up'. "During the winter ice cream didn't sell very well, so we sold sweets instead. Howard's made all their own sweets from the same premises as they made their ice cream on Mowbrey Street, Ashton." Incidentally Howard's also had a sweet stall within the indoor market for many years, and were of course the owners of the very popular Bow Street cafe. Besides the ice cream trailers there were other traders on the market who used similar vans. One was John Hulme & Son tripe dressers, and in 1952 they introduced to the market a new type of trailer. This anodised aluminium caravan stood the market ground everyday, and was the fourth in a fleet of mobile tripe shops owned by the Denton based company. The first of these caravans, which also traded at Bury, Bolton, Oldham and Hyde markets, was built in 1949. Mr. C.R. Langdon formerly chief sanitary inspector at Denton and now at this time assistant inspector at Ashton had been co-designer along with Mr. Hulme of the new trailers. The one at Ashton was built by the Coventry Steel Co. Ltd and the 16ft long trailer had windows made of quarter inch Perspex while its interior was lined with plastic, with the floor being of rubber bonded onto steel. Mr Hulme, who at this time was president of the North West area council of tripe dressers association believed that his van would help to establish a new standard in market trading. It was also in 1952 that the market ground itself took on a new look, when around £1,000 was spent on laying tarmac over the old existing cobbled surface. This was a major improvement which was certainly welcomed by both traders and shoppers alike who for years had suffered many a mishap and injury caused by the unevenness of the ground.

A busy market day c1952 - In the foreground (left to right) can be seen the trailers belonging to John Hulme & Son tripe dressers and the ice cream vendors Fairclough's and Howard's. To the left of the picture are the three roundabouts while just visible beyond are the kiddies swings.

Having previously taken a close look at Market Street, Bow Street and the Market Avenue at differing times, let us now stroll along the Warrington Street of the early 1950s. Starting from the Old Street end; and the Market House public house, from where the last pints were pulled in 1953. Next door was the rather imposing premises belonging to J. Andrew and Co. publishers of the Reporter group of newspapers, from here the town's longest serving paper was printed. The Reporter office loomed large over the market ground until the town centre redevelopment scheme of the 1960s. After the Reporter office, just across Cotton Street was the Ashton Hotel, another public house whose licensee at this time was Benjamin Downie. The first shop on this side of the street was Woods drapers.

The Reporter Office looming large over a 1950s market scene

Situated between this shop and the Katherine Street corner were the premises of George Marland undertaker, Avery Scales and Margaret's Hairdressers; Mrs. Howard's toffee shop and finally, Kilner's grocers. The latter left a lasting impression with us, for we can still recall that here was the first call made by our mother on our shopping trips. We can picture now its wooden floor, the wooden chair for weary customers with its metal advertising plate fixed to the backrest, it was for Camp Coffee. And coffee was just one of the smells which filled the air, all mixing together to give an aroma we can almost smell today. Upon the counter resting on a marble base was a huge round cheese which to us always seemed to be there, we often wondered if he ever sold any. Moving along, over Katherine Street and before reaching Wellington Road, you would pass a number of shops including Bob Fish butchers, George Byrom barber and perhaps one establishment which will be remembered by many, Sewell's chippy. There was also the Grapes public house, a record shop, false-teeth repair shop and the dress shop owned by Ann Moorecroft. On the opposite side, coming back towards the market ground, were a number of small retail outlets. These included a wallpaper shop, newsagents, pet shop, bakers, toffee shop and another chip shop, this one being owned by Knight's. Topham's clock shop was followed by the co-op wet fish shop. Proceeding along, before reaching the office of the Water Board, which was the last building before arriving at the market ground, you would pass a hairdressers, tobacconist, greengrocers, Rogerson's off license, a sweet shop and finally Bardsley's electrical shop. After the market ground itself, between Bow Street and Old Street, and taking up the whole block, was the very impressive looking George and Dragon public house.

The George & Dragon public House pictured from the corner of Bow Street and Warrington Street – After its closure the original beer cellars were transformed in to a new public house and in 2009 carried the name Oliver's Bar.

Perhaps one of the most well remembered of market superintendents over the years was Philip Poulter who held this position from 1955-1981. When Mr Poulter took over the job the outdoor market consisted of nine rows of stalls, with the last three rows being of the tubular steel variety. According to Mr Poulter, the market at this time was making a profit of around

£3,000 per annum. As for the traders, about one-third of those working outside were Jewish. There were only a very few coloured people on the market at this period, although one or two Asians were just beginning to trade. John Latus recalls; *"from being young I've seen many nationalities working on Ashton market and I can remember when the very first Asians appeared, mostly selling nylons from battered suitcases. I felt very protective towards them as they could speak very little English. These Asians were probably the first coloured people the townsfolk had seen, and as everyone knows, there was a lot of prejudice in those days. But that didn't stop the women buying their stockings from them, and they did very nicely. I found them very nice and polite and got on well with them ".*

In the early part of the 1950s one of Ashton market's most well known traders Harry Gilbert retired from his business. The art of pitching goods, of which Harry was a past master, was something that was still being carried out to some good effect by many other traders, as Mr Poulter recalls; *"A good market needs pitchers and one of the most notable from the 1950s was Abe Star another Jewish trader. Abe ran a sort of Dutch auction, but really he was trading on people's inherent greed of wanting something for nothing. He would start by offering items for about 3d or 6d, but when the crowd put up their hands for the goods he would not let them purchase them there and then, for to do so would mean he would lose his crowd. Instead he would say, 'right I know who you are', ensuring they would stay and by the time he had finished with his patter the public had spent more money than they had intended and more often than not on goods they didn't really want in the first place. In fact to me it just seemed as though he had them all mesmerised ".* Star has stayed in the memories of a lot of people, and one, Mrs Lillian Walker added: "*What impressed me most about Star were all those pound notes he had tucked into the band on his straw boater hat, such a sign of affluence in those days*". Mr Poulter continued; "*I used to get a lot of complaints about Star. People would come up to my office saying how they had been tricked into buying things. "I used to get the money back for some, but others deserved to have been taken for a ride*". One person, who really did take people for a ride in a way that would certainly not be allowed today, was the gentleman who displayed on his stall a very impressive looking aquarium containing a number of fish and

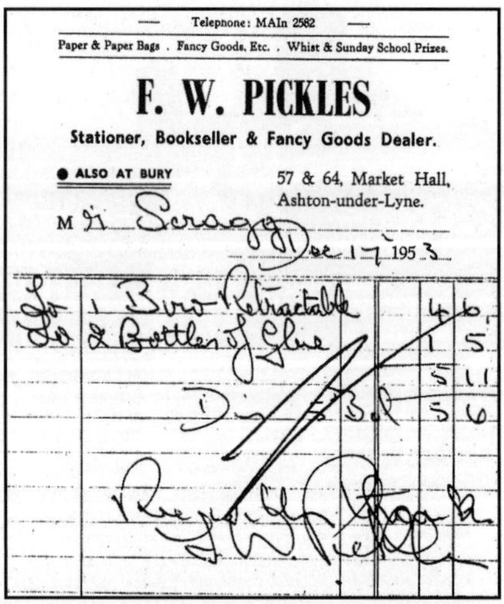
— Telephone: MAIn 2582 —

Paper & Paper Bags . Fancy Goods, Etc. . Whist & Sunday School Prizes.

F. W. PICKLES

Stationer, Bookseller & Fancy Goods Dealer.

● ALSO AT BURY

57 & 64, Market Hall,
Ashton-under-Lyne.

M Sr Scragg

Dec 17 1953

Mr Scragg, Market Superintendent and predecessor to Philip Poulter received a discount of 5d from F. W. Pickles on his purchases of 5s 11d in 1953

Another scene from the 1950s depicting a busy market ground

some magnificent 'Aqua Plants'. He would impress the crowd that he had gathered, with a speech on how these remarkable plants could be grown in any home tank, by using the 'Aqua Stones' he was selling at the so called 'amazingly low price' of just 2s 6d for three. Little did the public know that these intricate looking 'Aqua Stones' were no more than ordinary peach stones, which he had obtained free from a canning factory. Of course the ones in his tank had been 'doctored' somewhat with a pretty looking

Philip Poulter, Market Superintendent from 1955-1981 **(right)**
with Neville Morgan china and glassware dealer

flower or plant just stuck on to them. Another amusing tale recalled for us, concerns a trader who regularly worked Ashton market on Mondays. Dressed in cricket gear he would trade direct from his van, on the sides of which were placed two large boards containing photographs of him pictured with top cricketers of the time. From this pitch he would sell small round boxes containing a yellow cream which he claimed was an ointment to cure all aches and pains, implying at the same time that the same cream was used by the pictured sportsmen. He would ask if there was anyone within the crowd suffering from any muscular pain, and if so to step forward, and of course there was always someone who obliged. This person would then be sat down and as the trader began massaging the ointment upon the affected area, would simultaneously inform every one of its powers. It appears that the trader was quite a passable masseur and it is probably this fact alone that prompted most of the people who had come forward to say that they felt much better. The ointment may have had some pain relieving qualities that could have attributed to this, but it is very unlikely that it would have been so instant. The story goes that one Monday as he was having a particularly good day he realised that his stock would not last, and mentioned this fact to a fellow trader, adding if he knew where he could obtain some butter, it still being on ration at this time. Together they went to Shaw's grocers where his colleague knowing the shop proprietor managed to obtain an amount of butter by paying over the odds. On returning to his van on the market ground, our cricket attired friend immediately commenced to fill his empty ointment boxes with the butter, and shortly afterwards was facing a new crowd of shoppers, once again proclaiming its wonderful pain relieving qualities. Just how many people later that night were rubbing butter all over themselves saying 'that feels much better' is of course not known, but it's our guess that there might well have been one or two.

Amongst the many more reputable traders enjoying good business around this time were the long standing greengrocery concerns of Potter's and Kelly's. The second-hand furniture and bric-a-brac on the stall run Billy Parkin drew people around. Billy would clear houses after bereavements and had a warehouse on Victoria Street, and was a forerunner of today's flea market traders. Others were Lawrence Schofield selling overalls, Beeley's with new and second hand books, Mr and Mrs White with ladies clothing, Molly and Bill Jackson who came from Longsight to sell their children's wear and Queenie trading with Marks and Spencer's rejects. Many of the traders who stood the market around this time have remained in the memory of Ruth Rhodes née Latus – daughter of greengrocer John Latus snr. In her childhood the market was Ruth's playground and the stallholders were all like her 'aunties' and 'uncles'. Some of the pitchers would often use the services of Ruth to help them sell their wares. One in particular would 'select' her from the crowd to demonstrate the ease of use with the then new paint roller. 'If this little girl can use it so can you' he would say. Ruth was also well known to those with stalls in the indoor market, many of whom would in winter bring her inside to their stalls and the relative warmth of the market hall. Even after school Ruth would head for the family stall and hardly a day would pass without her being there at some point. It is hardly surprising therefore that just like her brother John (jnr) Ruth should follow in the family tradition by running a greengrocery stall of her own – which she continued with until 2004.

Cleaning work carried out during the late 1950s

By 1959 the market committee were pressing for approval for improvements to the covered market to be carried out, Philip Poulter said; *"at this time the hall had a huge coke burning boiler for the heating, and it wasn't a very good one at that, as most of the heat ended up in the roof and it took a whole day for it to come down. Which meant that it was warm by the time the hall was ready to close? The improvements when completed were far superior in that the building warmed up much quicker and the hot water which had previously been only available in the toilets was now being piped around to a good many stalls".* Other work carried out at this time included the installation of a public address system and the re-glazing of the lantern lights in the roof, while the old flagged floor was covered with a smoother asphalt surface. *"Before the floor was covered",* continued Mr Poulter; *"I was on occasions called back to the hall at night and I found myself walking on cockroaches, which were all over the floor having come up through the gaps between the old paving stones. You couldn't get at them to exterminate them, but with the new floor covering this problem did not arise, the cockroaches simply could not survive".*

During the spring of 1960 market day crowds often witnessed the sight of a somewhat overdressed 'gentleman of the road' strolling around the shopping area. He soon became a well noticed figure on the market ground as people were amazed to see a person wearing five overcoats and at least three pairs of trousers in such warm weather conditions. After sleeping out in the open countryside in nearby Park Bridge for a number of weeks, this tramp had now moved even closer to Ashton and had taken to venturing into the town centre, especially to the market where he hoped to obtain food. Over the weeks several stallholders had taken to offering him the occasional drink and biscuit which he eagerly accepted. One particular day when a trader asked if he would like to take a full packet of biscuits, he had no sooner answered yes before they had been consumed. Other stallholders hearing of this thought he must be starving and began to offer goods from their stalls. The speed at which he consumed these soon drew a big crowd around. They all stood watching with a mixture of curiosity and astonishment as he greedily ate a packet of Ryvita biscuits and a box of cheese, and the area was buzzing as he was passed two hands of bananas containing thirty-one bananas which were all consumed with apparent ease. A further seventeen bananas soon followed and then a specially made ice cream cone, the size of which would have filled a pint glass, this was washed down by a large bottle of lemonade, and finally before being given a cup of tea, he devoured a pound of pears. The public that were gathered could hardly believe the comment he made after finishing off his feast, when he was heard to say; *"I used to be able to eat once, that's been a real tonic to me".* As the crowd was beginning to disperse he was given four pies and four pounds of tomatoes. Two of the pies were eaten there and then, whilst the others, along with the tomatoes were placed in a bag for a meal later in the day. For many weeks after this event the public were used to seeing him on the market ground, and besides giving him food would shout; *"Hiya Banana Bill* " the name given to him by the local press on reporting of his initial remarkable feast. In July the town learned of his real identity under somewhat sad circumstances, after his body was found in Greenhurst Clough off Lees Road Ashton, his death had been caused by severe head injuries. He was 44 year old Thomas Henry Russell but to many townsfolk he was always remembered as Banana Bill.

As youngsters; there were many times, especially on Saturdays that we the authors, against our will would have joined our mother on her shopping expeditions, which always included a walk around Ashton market ground. Looking back at those trips, we recall that the walk around the stalls appeared to take forever, simply because we seemed to meet everyone mum knew, and of course she would have to stop and speak to them all. Overall the trips were not something we ever looked forward to. Unlike sometime later, especially between the years 1958 to 1962, when we made many trips to the market area together in order to spend our pocket money. We would start by buying sweets from Roy Hall's toffee stall; later of course he was to build up a flourishing wholesale cash and carry business. We would then look around at the various stalls before moving over to Stigwood's stall. He was the man who sold ex-juke box records and a good many of our collection played on the Dansette were purchased from him, simply because they were cheaper than buying new ones. When we did buy the new releases and chart records, or top twenty hits as they were known then, they were usually obtained from the long established Jones Music shop on Bow Street. Going into the market hall, via the entrance near to the top of the Market Avenue, there was situated to the left hand side Aldred's toy stall where at varying times due to our age difference, one or the other would obtain the latest model car from the Matchbox Series range. After this we would wander over to Pickles' whose stall along the one side displayed stationery and greetings cards, but it was the end facing Finnerty's cafe that interested us, for this was where a selection of jokes and tricks were on offer. On the other side of the stall were those wonderful American comics like Batman, Superman, Tales from the Crypt and Mad, all of them worth a thumb through even if we didn't always buy. Brown's toy stall was our next call to see if they had anything different or at least cheaper than the other similar stalls. Moving on through the crowds we arrived at Nadin's drink stall which sold a good selection of hot beverages and soft drinks, here it was decision time for us, was it to be milk shakes or pop perhaps a sarsaparilla. *"Oye, don't sit on the stall"* was a remark we often heard while drinking our pop, it came from someone working at Star Stores, the stall directly facing Nadin's. It seems as though not just us, but everyone would lean against their stall having obtained a drink. Of course that stall didn't interest us, just what did Oxydol do? There was a sweet stall in the market that we sometimes went to, was it still owned by Howard's at this time? It had a huge selection of sweets and chocolates all of which we thought a little expensive, so if anything was bought it was usually just a Knux or Tiffin. Before leaving the hall through the Wellington Road door, there was usually time for a glance at the English comics over at Hindle's newsagents, prior to catching the number 7 bus home from the stop at the side of the market.

Austin Stigwood and his wife Barbara are still remembered by many people who visited the market on the busy Saturdays to buy their ex-juke box records. Austin recalled; *"We stood Ashton Market for over twenty-three*

Ah memories ... the number 7 bus to the Crowhill Estate would soon have us home after our childish jaunts around the market.

years, during which time we met and became friends with a great many people and indeed got to know a few of the market characters. Such a one was an elderly gentleman called 'Joe' - we never knew his last name - but on cold days he would suddenly appear as if from nowhere, brandishing a flask of hot tea, and cream crackers and cheese. I can tell you tea has never tasted so good. Selling records as we did, we met a variety of people, with varied musical tastes. There was one young couple who were Elvis fans, who would request we play a few Elvis records. Within minutes they would move to the space at the side of the stall and begin to jive, they were then quickly joined by others. Of course all this attracted the attention of the crowds which meant good business for us and also good fun". Of course these weren't the only Elvis fans to visit the Stigwood stall, for apparently one young woman would stand quietly to one side listening to Elvis singing '*Old Shep*', however, she never bought anything but would always go away with her eyes full of tears. Christmas for many traders was always a time of anxiety, especially about the weather, with all hoping that it would stay fine enabling them to clear out their extra Christmas stock. With quite a bit of stock still left on their hands as a particular Christmas was approaching, the Stigwood's could ill afford any congestion around their stall, as Austin recalls; *"It was almost Christmas time and we were busy on the stall, when my wife, Barbara, looked up and saw the face of actress Pat Phoenix, then known to millions of television viewers as Elsie Tanner of Coronation Street. Well, without a moments hesitation Barbara was around the front of the stall to greet her with the words 'Eee Elsie it's really nice to see you, now do me a favour and bugger off before anyone sees you'. A few days later my wife wrote to her apologising, and explained how we didn't want the congestion around the stall to kill off the business.*

Pat happily understood the reasoning and assured my wife not to worry about it. As time went on Pat Phoenix became a regular and valued customer, as well as a friend."

The name 'Queenie' was synonymous with Ashton's indoor market, and had been ever since 1962 when Queenie moved inside after serving the public for over twenty-five years from a position on the market ground. Her full name was Queenie Jones and it had been with her mother that she began working on the markets at Ashton and Stalybridge. In her early years Queenie would take in the two markets on the same day, starting at Stalybridge at 5am until 10am then moving on to Ashton where she worked up until 9pm. Crowds at both the markets would be in waiting for her to arrive and no sooner had her clothing stock been placed on the sheeting, than it was eagerly snapped up, she never had anything left by the close of day. In time Queenie progressed to an actual stall on the market ground and the business continued to flourish. On eventually moving inside, her husband remained on the outdoor market, but it wasn't long before the decision to give up the outside pitch altogether was taken.

Visit Queenie's New Stall
IN THE ASHTON COVERED MARKET
GRAND OPENING SALE
Bargains in Italian and Scotch Knitwear
Banlon Cardigans and Jumpers in the very latest styles.
Famous brands in Fancy Nylon Underskirts and Nylon and Cotton Nighties

The year is 1962 and 'Queenie' moves her 'Royal' residence from market ground to market hall.

The face of town centre Ashton was to change dramatically over the next decade when under a major slum clearance scheme the rows of terraced houses of Charlestown were demolished to make way for the town's first bus-station. What had been the site of shops and houses stretching back to Gas Street from Wellington Road was soon to be occupied by a new shopping precinct. Prior to all this however, there were to be major changes ahead for the market area. As these changes were to go far beyond just plain improvements the council had engaged Professor Denis Harper, of the Manchester College of Science and Technology, as a consultant. Indeed it was Professor Harper who came up with a plan that was to totally redevelop Ashton Market. His plan when put to the market traders, during 1960 was met with much enthusiasm; he explained that there was to be no question of interfering with the essential initial character of the market ground. He added however, that it did need improving in colour, in scheme and in order. In his opinion the market hall was a very good building that with care could, along with its tower, be made something worth looking at. By the autumn of 1962 all the work entailed in bringing the Professor's plans to fruition were completed. Chaumont Way the new colourfully paved walkway leading across the front of the market hall, from the Market Avenue to the front of the town hall, was the first section to be officially opened, with the honour being undertaken by Monsieur Marcel a civic dignitary from Chaumont, Ashton's French twinned town.

When the market itself was officially opened in October by Harvey Rhodes MP, many new features and improvements were evident, the front of the market hall and its clock tower had both been cleaned and were now adorned with decorative lighting. Five 30ft lamp standards ran along the side of the hall facing the market ground. Incidentally the stalls themselves had now been changed to run east to west as opposed to north to south New lighting on these along with brightly covered awnings vastly improved their appearance. A contemporary styled ice cream kiosk stood adjacent to a St. John's ambulance station both situated immediately in front of the market building in the shadow of the clock tower. Further kiosks were situated at the bottom of the market at both Bow Street and Katherine Street sides. There were four separate units selling tea, sandwiches, tripe and ice cream housed in the Oriental style kiosk at the Bow Street side, while a smaller kiosk for the sale of ice creams was situated near to the children's roundabouts at the corner of Katherine Street. These roundabouts were newly sited in a safe walled area in which was also included a number of seats from where parents could keep a watchful eye on their children. Further seating was also available for weary shoppers to rest within another walled area in a terraced enclosure on Chaumont Way. Katherine Street had now been closed off to traffic from its junction with Warrington Street at its one end and Wellington Road at the other. This made the market a little safer for the shoppers with now no fear of speeding traffic. Work had also been undertaken to the town hall which further enhanced the area, sandblasting had given the civic building a whole newer clean appearance and entrance to it was now gained by ascending a new shallower double flight of steps. Newly planted trees made the area a much more pleasant place to shop and the total cost for the refurbishments had cost in the region of £21,000. As a direct consequence of these improvements the rents for stalls both in the market hall and those on the market ground were increased. However, unlike the previous occasion there were no complaints for as one tenant at the time said; *"We have been given the rights to sell our businesses which we did not have before, we knew rents would have to go up because of the improvements made".* The right to sell businesses only applied to the tenants at the market hall, who had seen their rents raised from 3d to 6d per superficial foot.

The rearrangement of the stalls that had taken place resulted in all of the greengrocery businesses being placed together in one line, which ran along the Bow Street side of the ground. Prior to this all the fruit and vegetable stalls had been spread out around the square in various positions. The opinions of many people though, was that when the stalls were scattered around the market prices were more competitive. Shoppers were inclined

Two pictures showing Ashton's new 1960s style market with most stalls now running east to west – note also the Oriental style kiosks

to walk around them all checking for the cheapest. In doing so they would pass the stalls of other traders which could result in more business for them. Mr Poulter said; *"one reason for having all these stalls together was to keep all their rubbish in one part of the market instead of it being all over the place, but I do agree that having the stalls spread out meant varying prices ".*

The positioning of all the fruit and vegetable stalls together may well have made things a little easier for one of the market characters who had become a familiar figure to the public and traders, as she daily for many years would regularly collect and break up for firewood, the wooden boxes left by the market greengrocers. To many of the traders she was simply known as Lizzie, for very few knew her full name or anything about her. Dressed in a crumpled top coat and ankle length skirt, Lizzie also wearing her familiar beret and mittens was easily recognisable as she wheeled her battered old pram, on which she had piled and secured the boxes. Unfortunately the impression, quite wrongly gained by many was that Lizzie was either a vagrant or simply a poor old lady who had to eke out a living selling firewood. Both, however, were far from the truth, Lizzie or to use her full name Elizabeth Thornton came from Quaker stock and her father during his working life would stand outside the local workhouse and give over to the poor one-third of his wage. He brought Lizzie up to believe that the only way to give anyone anything was to suffer oneself in the process. Throughout her life this was something that Lizzie always maintained and for a total of 47 years she would walk to Salford where she worked in a cotton mill, money was also saved by denying herself a lunch and then these savings she would pass on to someone she thought was in greater need, doing so she felt she had done something worthwhile. Having never married, Lizzie lived most of her life at her parents' house on Brassey Street, Ashton, where in later life she took care of her aging mother until she died in her mid-80s. After the death of her mother, the house was left to Lizzie's sister-in-laws, her brothers having been killed during the war. Not receiving anything from the eventual sale of the house she was forced to move into

'Lizzie' (Elizabeth Thornton) carrying out her daily routine of collecting firewood

one of the bungalows reserved for older residents at Ashurst Gardens, Ashton.

Living alone Lizzie continued her daily routine of collecting wood from the market and it wasn't uncommon for her to be seen still breaking up the wood at 10 o'clock at night. She had a regular clientele all too willing to buy her bundles of firewood. All the money she raised from its sale would be given to a local charity or church. Gathering all the wood wasn't quite as straightforward as most people thought, for she would not just take the wood, though many traders offered it, instead Lizzie preferred to earn the wood by doing little jobs. She was not much of a conversationalist though she was very polite and would always answer a 'good morning' with an equally civil response. One person with whom she did converse was greengrocer John Latus, who also befriended her and became very close. Mr Latus recalled; *"she was a very devout Catholic, though her Quaker upbringing remained, and she continued to live a life of self denial. She only ever drank water no tea or coffee, and to save water she would only flush her toilet once a day. If I ever wanted to send her an errand I had to be very careful on where I wanted her to go, because if I gave her bus fare she would probably walk instead and save the money to give to someone else".* When the time came that Lizzie couldn't look after herself any longer John Latus and his wife offered their help and spent a good deal of time in trying to find a suitable residential home, where she could be looked after and cared for. After enquiring all over Tameside their search failed to find accommodation for Lizzie and unfortunately, after spending all her life in Ashton she had to move into a home in Oldham where she spent the remainder of her life. John Latus says: *"I felt very sad about that, for after being in Ashton for her whole life and after doing so much good for the local people no where could be found for her".* Before her death Lizzie left in the possession of John Latus a letter containing her wishes and arrangements upon her death. Among things stated in the letter was her feeling that there should be no mourners, or graveside agony as she called it, and nothing was to be published in the Reporter, she added that she was aware that if she hadn't been a good person in life then she wouldn't get into heaven. John Latus somewhat emotionally added; *"Miss Elizabeth Thornton was a marvellous character and one who made a great impression on my life, I do hope there is a heaven for she literally dedicated her life to doing good".*

In November of 1966 market traders and public alike mourned the death of Florrie Waters owner of Finnerty's cafe, where she had worked for 45 years. Florrie's son John Finnerty inherited the business and continued with the same traditions that the cafe had become renowned for. The big potato pie remained as popular as ever and the customers still queued at dinnertime for the freshly sliced pork.

At various times throughout the history of Ashton's market ground there have been a number of traders whom the public have looked upon with great affection. During the 1960s stallholder Abraham Bland, known to everyone as 'Aby', was to join this select group. The reason why Aby was held in such high esteem was to become evident as Christmas approached. For a good many years at Christmas time Aby had arranged for food parcels to be made up which he gave out to the old folk of the town. However, in 1966 he had a different treat in store when he invited two-hundred Old Aged Pensioners to a party in the Town Hall. Aby and his wife enlisted the help of the WRVS to serve the food which included fresh sandwiches, fruit, trifle and cakes. The party got underway with several games including bingo which proved to be the most popular. No expense was spared as Aby also gave everyone a propelling pencil and a pound box of chocolates, with the ladies also receiving a special gift of a brooch. One can hardly imagine any stallholder today doing anything like this.

Around this period developments were taking place which on completion would not only change the face of town centre Ashton but also the shopping habits of the public. At various stages several properties along Bow Street were demolished to make way for new retail outlets including a 'Savemore' supermarket. However, it would be the development on the Old Street and Warrington Street area which would have the greatest impact on the town's future as a shopping centre - For here a traffic-free shopping precinct would shortly bring many new and major retailers in to town. In April 1967 the North Western Electricity Board moved out of their showroom, which had been situated in the old fish market section of the market hall, to become one of the first traders in the new shopping precinct. They were soon to be followed by the likes of Tesco supermarket and many more 'High Street' names.

Part of the new shopping precinct as it was in 1967 with the North West Electricity Board in the background. Today as the Ladysmith Centre it has been much altered.

New laws introduced around this time now prevented the sale of certain food stuffs upon the market ground, other than under strict conditions set out by the new regulations regarding hygiene. In order to sell such items as meats, poultry, unwrapped bakery, unwrapped sweets and cooked meats, all stalls had now to have hot water and separate sinks, both for staff and for washing utensils. Unable to meet these new requirements on the open market ground the need for a purpose built food hall was discussed and the former electricity showroom was suggested would make the ideal premises. With the go-ahead given, Peter Binns working for Ashton Corporation was the man responsible for the design and supervision of this new food hall, the construction of which began in January 1968. A total of £22,000 was spent on the work, which included new fluorescent lighting, a new drainage system and tiled floor. A new upper floor was added to allow for badly needed storage room with space left available for the addition of a gent's staff toilet. Eighteen stalls were fitted five of which were double units, these stood in two rows running down either side of the hall, all units were fitted with sinks and hot water, and most also had refrigerators installed. Entrance to the food hall was gained either from doors at the Wellington Road side of the building or from the door facing the open market, this being the now reopened entrance to the old fish market. The removal of an existing stall from within the market hall itself facilitated easy access directly from the covered market area.

During the early 1960s, before the opening of the 'Savemore' supermarket on Bow Street and Tesco's in the new £3million shopping precinct, the town had been served by only a couple of small supermarkets which were really nothing more than self-serve shops. For many people shopping for everyday foodstuffs was still carried out from the grocers and provisions shops, of which there were a good many in and around the market area. Tinned foods could be bought from at least three stalls on the market ground, the new indoor foodhall was selling everything from bread to meat, while the main market hall still had many established food stalls continuing to serve the public. The Co-op on its grocery stall sold mainly their own branded goods and to some people 'Waveney Beans', '99 Tea' or 'Willowvale Cheese Spread' were a must, while their 'Wheatsheaf Bread' and other bakery items were available from their nearby bread stall. A popular provisions stall was Redman's where bacon and cheeses could be obtained. They were also noted for a range of potted meats and fish spread, and a second stall sold tinned and packet foods. Another similar stall was that of E. Lowe who also sold farm-fresh eggs as well as loose butter beans, dried peas and other various pulses all of which were scooped out of large green metal containers that stood directly in front of the stall. Situated near to Lowe's were two tripe stalls one belonging to U.C.P who also had larger premises on George Street. Although still having their regular customers, the days of tripe being a good selling commodity had now passed by. There may well have been a decline in street corner butchers shops, and indeed those within the market hall had also declined in total over the years, but there was still quite a number who had built up and maintained good trade, some that readily spring to mind are David Conn, The Co-op, Briggs, and Ashworth's. Two local bakeries A. Lees of Queens Road, and F. Oldfield of Cockbrook both had outlets within the market hall for the sale of their bread and cakes. Oldfield's long established in the market occupied a large square stall with service obtainable from any one of its four sides. While most of the market's fruit and vegetable trade was conducted on the outdoor market, a smaller number did operate inside; these included once again the Co-op, Walkers, Walters and Sowerbutt's salad stall. Vera Shevlin was at this period beginning what would be twenty years working in the market hall. Vera remembered her first job was part-time on Sowerbutt's stall where she washed lettuce, trimmed celery as well as serving the public. *"All the staff had to be called by their surnames and the customers addressed as sir or madam, there was no calling them love".* Vera also spoke of the great friendship that existed between the staff from all the stalls and of the many parties which were organised – especially those at Christmas held at the George and Dragon on Bow Street. After four years on the salad stall Vera switched to the vegetable stall of Jim Walker which was situated near to the Co-op butchers, *"Jim was a lovely man to work for and later the stall was taken over by Alan Walker"* she revealed. After deciding to work full-time Vera found herself next employed at Lowe's Bacon stall. Lowe's was managed by Alma Bates who was known to everyone for the way she could slice bacon into thin rashers and apparently was also a wizard at boning hams.

Vera Shevlin pictured at Sowerbutt's salad stall 1965

On the outdoor market the early part of 1968 had seen a handful of traders being allowed onto the market ground on the non-market days of Wednesdays and Thursdays. These few traders, who were dealing mainly in second hand goods, were given the privilege of a reduced rent, something which traders on the official market days were not too pleased with. They voiced their opinion in July by which time the supposedly non-market days had seen even more stalls introduced and fairly large crowds being attracted to them. It was troubling the regular Monday, Friday and Saturday tenants that the increasingly busy Wednesday and Thursdays were starting to take trade away from them, there was just not enough money around to support a five day week market they said. The council however, encouraged by the way extra rents were being taken now had ideas of officially making the market into a five day one. Angry traders seeing what similar moves like this had done for other North West towns handed in a petition. One irate stallholder stated; *"In towns where five day trading has been introduced the market had deteriorated rapidly".* They were also unhappy about the quality of goods being sold on these days, another trader angrily pointed out that it was nothing but junk and something which should not be allowed especially in sight of the new multi-million pound shopping precinct. Over the next few months during which the five day trading continued, the council had discussions regarding the issue and eventually in October they said that from now the market for a six month trial period, will become a five day week market, with Wednesdays and Thursdays being available for all businesses that wished to trade on these days. After the trial period had expired, Mr. Philip Poulter market superintendent said: *"winter is always a testing time but the average number of stalls occupied was quite good. It is probably the only market in the north to have a successful outdoor market five days a week".* He added that the outdoor market would in his opinion go from strength to strength, something which the passing of time has proved to be correct.

CHRISTMAS SHOPPING IN ASHTON'S MARKET HALL

TAYLOR MAID FASHIONS

FOR THE BEST CHOICE OF

★ Kilts from 29/11 ★ Skinny Ribs 32/6

★ Tent Dresses 55/- ★ Hipsters from 19/11

★ Fashion Knitwear 24/11

34 MARKET HALL, ASHTON-UNDER-LYNE

Best-Quality Turkeys our Speciality

Christmas Orders taken now !

W. BRIGGS

BUTCHER

MARKET HALL, ASHTON (Tel. ASH 1466)

GRADE 'A' MEAT ONLY. QUALITY FIRST!

C. BROWNE (ESTABLISHED)

JEWELLERY AND FANCY GOODS

Largest selection in the district of

Brooches, Ear-Rings, Necklets, Lockets, Crosses and Chains, Leather Goods, etc.

• COME AND SEE OUR SELECTION — IDEAL FOR CHRISTMAS GIFTS

HARTLEY'S

YOUR 'LADYBIRD' CENTRE for Ideal Gifts

"Ladybird" Wool/Fibro/Mohair DRESSES Age 2—10 e.g. Age 4 25/11	"Ladybird" DRESSING GOWNS Cotton Washable. Age 2's—8's e.g. 2 years 28/11 Courtelle / Cotton. Easy-Dry 2's—8's e.g. Age 4 36/11

For Children	Gifts for Men	For Her
Pyjamas, Sleeping Suits, Brushed Nylon Nightgowns, Sweaters, Trews, Shorts	Pullovers, Cardigans, Waistcoats, Dressing Gowns, Scarves	Quilted Nylon Housecoats Nightgowns Bed Jackets Gloves

QUALITY — HARTLEY'S — VALUE

A HAT

makes all the difference

Good selection of Children's Knitted Caps and Children's Wear

ROSE WALLWORK Millinery and Drapery

38 MARKET HALL, ASHTON-UNDER-LYNE

BAILEYS HARDWARE

LIMITED

★ FANCY GOODS, TOYS, READING LAMPS, RUGS, MATS, KITCHENWARE, ELECTRIC LIGHT FITTINGS

★ GOODS LAID BY ALL THE YEAR ROUND CLUB

S. WALKER & SONS

(A-u-L) LTD., MARKET HALL, ASHTON

FINEST DISPLAY OF FRUIT, FLOWERS & VEGETABLES

• We specialise in our own grown produce direct from Nurseries Telephone ASHton 5803 or DROylsden 1148 •

WHY NOT PAY A VISIT TO

VANITY FAIR

(Prop. Lilian Dawson)

for COSMETICS, TOILET GOODS, etc.

Also CHRISTMAS GOODS on show at reasonable prices

All good makes in stock and served "always with a smile"

Exquisite BONE CHINA

FULL RANGE OF FINE GLASSWARE including Colclough Replaceable Bone China. Seven delightful patterns

Full stock of PYREX WARE, JUNE ROSE, GAIETY, MATCHMAKER and new KENT ORCHARD

• All useful, acceptable Christmas Gifts at —

BATES & MARSH Market Hall, Ashton

FOR QUALITY AND SERVICE

E. LOWE & SON

THE GROCERS

42 MARKET HALL ASHTON

•

Finest Danish Bacon sliced specially for you

Extra Selected Cheshire Cheese and Farm-Fresh New-Laid Eggs

ALSO AT HYDE SUPERMARKET

TASTY PASTRIES...

and the best BREAD are supplied by us in a big way. Deal with a baker who deals with us, and you'll never 'bake' a mistake

Birthday and Wedding Cakes made to order

Canteens and Cafes supplied

Visit our stall in Ashton Market Hall for all your Bread, Confectionery and Pies

F. OLDFIELD LTD.

Wholesale Bakers and Confectioners

Rutland St., Ashton-u Lyne Tel. ASHton 1940

Selected Fruit | **J. WALTERS** | Home-Grown Salads

HIGH CLASS FLORIST

Orders made up by artist in floral design. The choicest blooms selected

WORLD-WIDE TELEFLOWER SERVICE

(7 days a week Free Delivery Service)

Largest Selection of Frozen Foods | Market Hall, Ashton-u-Lyne Tel. ASH 1180 Also at Richmond Park Estate, Ashton | Your Garden Requirements

---

If FOOD Is Your Requirement

THE "CO-OP STALLS"

Will give you satisfaction

FRESH MEAT

GROCERIES

CONFECTIONERY

COOKED MEATS

GREENGROCERY

FLOWERS FOR THE OCCASION

STOCKINGS

HEAPS

CURTAINING

HEAPS

TABLECLOTHS

HEAPS

MEN'S SOCKS

HEAPS

CHRISTMAS GIFTS

CASSONS

Footware Specialists

See our extensive range of PIRELLI SLIPPERS

84-86 Penny Meadow Ashton. Tel: 1552

The Market Hall Ashton

Several market hall businesses advertising their wares for Christmas 1966

Chapter Five.

To market, to market to buy a plum cake,
back again, back again, baby is late;
To market, to market to buy a plum bun,
back again, back again market is done.

Ashton Market Ground 1991

The development of the new shopping precinct had begun to have an effect on Stamford Street as Ashton's main shopping high street. Meetings were held between the development company, Metrolands Investments and the Chamber of Trade, who both admitted that the number of empty shops on Stamford Street was becoming something of a concern. However, at the time, despite the arrival of the precinct it was believed that Stamford Street would still attract a lot of shoppers – time sadly proved this not to be the case. Once fully opened retailers in the precinct included names such as Curry's, Radio Rentals, Timpson's Shoes, Dewhurst Butchers, Crown Wallpapers, Warburton's Confectionary and of course Tesco. The likes of Mark's & Spencer and Woolworth's would also shortly herald their arrival in town directly opposite the open market on Warrington Street.

With the arrival of the supermarkets many businesses from the market were affected. Ken Rogerson, who at this time owned an off licence on Warrington Street, realised that if Tesco and Savemore were to be granted licenses to sell beers, wines and spirits, then his own business would suffer. He successfully managed to block their initial applications, but knowing that it was only a temporary measure and that they would continually reapply until they were successful, decided to play the supermarkets at their own game. The premise that the supermarkets followed was that everything that the housewife needed, including beers, wines and spirits, should be available under one roof. With this in mind Mr Rogerson thought that if he had an outlet in the market hall then surely the same argument would apply. After seeking advice on the matter he sought out a suitable stall and was fortunate in acquiring the business of a shoe retailer, which being housed in one of the brick built outlets was ideally suited for conversion to an off licence. Mr Rogerson's application for a license was heard by the magistrates at the same time as those put forward by Tesco and Savemore. All three applications were successful but Mr Rogerson was still to have problems. For although the market committee had no objections for the change of use for the stall, from shoes to alcohol it seems as though the rest of the council did. There were to be a further two applications put to the council before he eventually succeeded. After installing all the essential security systems Mr Rogerson opened his off licence stall in 1969. Having an off licence in a market hall seems to have been unique at this time for according to the trade representatives that Mr Rogerson dealt with, none knew of any other. Although it did take some time for the new outlet to become established it eventually built up a thriving business. In its early days, the off licence found great popularity amongst members of the town's Polish community. For some time Mr Rogerson had been asked by them if he could supply certain Polish vodkas which at the time they found difficult to obtain. Unfortunately this was something that Mr Rogerson couldn't do, until he happened to come into contact with an exiled Pole who was just beginning to import some in small quantities. Having a stock of vodkas the names of which he couldn't pronounce attracted good business from the Polish people. Many of them would gather near to the stall on a Saturday morning having purchased their favourite tipple and would stay happily chatting to one another in their native tongue for quite some considerable time.

Tennis players pose with Mr and Mrs Rogerson in a promotion for local heats of the Dewar Cup in 1970. Tickets were given free with purchases of Dewar's Whisky.

The 1960s had seen a great number of changes in fashions and fads and to keep up to date many stalls brought in new lines or even a completely different range of products. The simple plastic flower had become for a time the new 'in thing' and was given away by nearly every petrol company, washing powder manufacturer and coffee producer. The wide availability of these seems to have had its effect, with almost every housewife either buying or collecting them. This, perhaps surprisingly was being felt by the local florist trade, as if competition from rivals wasn't enough to cope with, a plastic flower was too much. Seeing a decline in his own flower sales John Walters, who had taken over the indoor market stall after the death of his father, 'Banana King' Harry Walters, decided to dispense with the florist part of the business. John Walters recalled:

Walters' greengrocers stall during the late 1960s – Items for sale include best salad tomatoes at 1s 6d (7½p) per pound and beetroot at 1s (5p) per pound.

"After that side of the business slowed down I changed it over to market gardening, and following on from that I introduced cacti and probably had the finest shows of cacti gardens this town has ever seen. These gardens were marvellous things set on dishes, and I enjoyed a good trade with these for about four or five years before it started to drop off. If a thing didn't go I wasn't afraid to clear it out and start on something new; although the greengrocery side of the business was and had always remained steady." "With the cacti gone I now turned to the mushroom trade and for a while the sale of mushrooms was booming and I had five staff on a Saturday selling nothing but these". "Eventually even these sales waned, so I took them off, just keeping a few with the greengrocery side. In their place I began trading with frozen foods and was the first to do so in the inside market". As opposed to the supermarkets and large shops whose frozen food was of the packaged variety John Walters sold his frozen food loose. His aim was to cater for the needs of those people on

low incomes, single people and simply those who only required just one item or a small quantity. Mr Walters was obviously meeting the needs of many, for as his business increased he started more staff and installed additional freezers. This type of business was later carried out elsewhere in the market hall by Polar Pantry occupying the stall that had once belonged to Brown's toy stall and afterwards by The Ice Box in the Food Hall. At the time that Mr Walters decided to retire from the market his frozen food sales had become the main part of his business outstripping the takings from the greengrocery side, finishing up as he did with ten freezers. On his retirement during the 1970s the stall was acquired by Casson's shoe retailers who already had one stall in the market hall and a shop on Penny Meadow.

Another stall which changed hands in the 1970s was 'Star Stores' which traded in household supplies, and was owned at the time by a Mr Hutchinson. The new owners were now Colin and Lesley Booth whom on taking over the business found most of their trade was coming from the older generation. In catering for this, it became common practice for them to split open the blocks of washing soap, Sunlight, Lifebuoy and the like, enabling the OAPs to purchase just the one tablet. Also high on their customers shopping lists was 'Dolly Cream' and 'Dolly Blue', while many shoppers still visited the stall for 'Donkey Stones'. For those to young to remember, 'Dolly Blue' was an aid to washing whites and linen and supposedly gave added brightness. Although the Booth's hardly changed anything at the stall during their ownership, they did introduce one innovation in the form of a one-hour photo processing machine, a first for the market hall. The stall did eventually take on a new look, bringing it more up to date when the Booth's successors J & L Bargains revamped it changing it over to a self service walk-round unit. The humble 'Donkey Stone' as sold by the Booth's deserves a fuller explanation; for at one time this was a product used by almost every housewife especially those in the north of the country. These stones which were made from sandstone, cement, bleach and water were originally made to supply a non-slip surface on the stone staircases of northern cotton mills. However, the house-proud womenfolk were soon using them for cleaning their own doorsteps and windowsills. When the Booth's acquired the stall there remained only one major manufacturer of 'Donkey Stones' in the country this being the local firm of Eli Whalley. Founded in the 1890s the company produced 2.5million stones a year during the heydays of the 1930s. In 1973 Gilbert Garside took over the business which was still based at premises at the canal side on Lower Wharf Street, Ashton. The stones derived their name from the Donkey trademark of Edward Read & Son of Manchester one of the earliest firms to produce them and those produced by Eli Whalley carried their mark of 'Lion Brand'. At one time Donkey Stones were obtained from the rag and bone man or totter in exchange for old clothing – don't remember the rag and bone man? If you've ever seen TVs 'Steptoe & Son' then that's your rag and bone man. When Gilbert

Garside finally ceased trading in 1979 the Booth's who still had a small but loyal trade for the stones came to an agreement whereby the machinery needed for their manufacture was leased to them – thus enabling production to be maintained until eventually demand for the stones had almost ceased. Eli Whalley's original machinery as used by Garside's and latterly the Booth's in producing this uniquely northern product is now housed in the Portland Basin Heritage Centre. In 2000 Tameside MBC erected a Blue Plaque commemorating Eli Whalley at what was formerly Ashton Old Wharf now renamed Donkey Stone Wharf. Surprisingly even as we entered the new millennium trade for donkey stones had not totally diminished as Bailey's Hardware stall within the indoor market was still offering them for sale at 65p each. In 2003 Gerald Buckley owner of the stall said, *"We still have people coming in here asking for them, especially people living in the old weaver type cottages in Mossley and Glossop".* The supplies now came from Colne in Lancashire where one man continued to produce unbranded stones from his garden shed.

An original 'Lion Brand' Donkey Stone as produced by Eli Whalley.

The running of Ashton market took on a whole new and different administration during 1974 when the town along with eight of its neighbours amalgamated to form the new larger Borough of Tameside. Under this new council all the markets within Tameside came under the control of one department, which today is the Estates and Industrial Development Department. Ashton no longer had its own market superintendent; instead there was now one principal markets officer who was based in the market office within the Ashton market clock tower.

During the first few days of January 1976 parts of Britain were caught up in hurricane force winds which caused many thousands of pounds worth of damage and tragically caused 22 deaths, though fortunately none locally. Throughout the night of Friday 2nd January into the early hours of Saturday winds of up to 80mph left a trail of destruction through Ashton, Dukinfield and Audenshaw. In Ashton town centre part of the gable end to 'Wild's Pet Shop' on Warrington Street was blown down while windows were smashed and other damage caused at Woolworths', 'The Wooden Spoon Café', 'The Sleep Centre' and 'Flanagan & Brookes'. Several stalls on Ashton open market ground were blown over with one actually finishing up at the top of the town hall steps. The roundabout once owned by Nora Rust and now being run by her son Fred and his wife Barbara ended up as a twisted wreck. The kiddies ride was an old fashioned one unlike those seen today, and being a massive structure and very heavy, its own weight toppled it in the force of the wind. Barbara Rust always maintained that of the three roundabouts theirs was the most open to the elements and the coldest spot on the market. As a consequence of the damage the ride had to be totally reconstructed a task which was undertaken at the market garden belonging to Barbara's brother, John Latus at Ashton Moss. Most of the toys which the children sat on and many of the specialised parts needed for the rides had to be brought up from London as there were none available locally. Eventually with the job completed the 'new' ride was back sitting proudly in place beside the other roundabouts belonging to the Seldon's. The Rusts and the Seldon's had always been friends and when needed would help each other – in business it was still a friendly rivalry. However, with the arrival of the Rust's 'new' ride the friendship seemed to wane, Barbra recalled; *"It seemed as though they did not want to know when we rebuilt our ride, they didn't like the idea it had been rebuilt because I suppose they thought it was now obviously better than theirs. Children would actually wait to go on ours".* Barbara Rust would often tell stories to the children about the horses and cars and other toys that used to be on the old ride – she had a genuine interest in the youngsters who all used to call her 'Old Tight'. The name came from when Barbara used to shout 'Hold Tight' as the ride began to go around. *"Many times when in Ashton, young children out with their mums would say 'look there's 'Old Tight'",* recalled Barbara.

Left to Right: ***The roundabouts owned by Mary Seldon, John Seldon and the Fred Rust. The latter having been rebuilt in 1976***

1976 saw Roy Smith applying for and obtaining the position of Assistant Market Manager after becoming a casualty of Britain's collapsing engineering industry. One of the tasks performed by Roy was to ensure the market hall was secure at the end of each trading day. Roy recalled *"In the course of only the first few weeks of my working in the markets and in the midst of a prolonged hot dry spell, I secured the hall in the evening, but inadvertently overlooked closing the electrically operated roof ventilator shutters". Each one provided an opening of about 36inches by 18inches and there were around forty to fifty of them altogether". That night the area suffered its heaviest downpour for months". I was eventually forgiven by some very understanding traders".* During the late 1970s following a spate of overnight break-ins at the market hall a highly sophisticated alarm system was installed. This intruder detection devise comprised of electronic beams which were transmitted wall to wall and down alleyways adjacent to the frontage of the stalls. Being among the designated key holders registered with the local police for any night time emergency call outs Roy was occasionally awakened from his sleep. One particular Friday morning around 2.15am he received a call from the police asking him to make his way to the hall as the alarm was sounding. On his arrival Roy together with the police inspected the exterior of the building for signs of any break-in. With all the windows and doors appearing secure the party entered the hall. Mr Smith silenced the alarm and along with the police began a tour of inspection the conclusion of which saw everything in order. As he was about to re-secure the building and switch off the lights he suddenly saw the cause of the problem. This was summertime and it had been an exceptionally hot day. A florist had left several buckets of quite tall stems of gladioli at the front of his stall. Several of these flowers had wilted and in doing so had passed through the detector beam triggering the alarm. Roy remembers, *"Mr 'Florist' was, the next day requested to adjust his practices so that I might enjoy a good night's sleep.*

Over the years the market has had a reputation for providing a variety of goods from clothing to housewares, electrical to furnishings and from food to horticultural. Looking at just one single row of stalls during this period in the 1970s, could be seen such diverse lines as Ken's Coats, Beth's cushion foam and leatherette fabrics, Edie Ryder's material stall along with Jim and Helen Patterson's ladies knitwear. One stall we the authors remember well was 'Disc Stop' a record stall run by a gentleman named Jeff where Soul and Motown records could be purchased – those that other record shops never seemed to stock. Avid book readers may well recollect Beeley's new and second hand book stall who since the mid-1950's had provided reading matter on a number of subjects. It was on this family run stall in 1977 that nine-year-old Jason Beeley first entered the wonderful world of the market trader. Jason worked before and after school 3 to 4 days a week until school leaving age. For one so young it was hard and heavy work especially when having to pull trolleys loaded with books from the storeroom at the rear of the Pitt and Nelson Public House – where once the dray horses were housed. *"It was really hard then",* recalled Jason, *"especially pulling the trolley over the cobbled stones, even harder when snow and ice was on the ground and my hands nearly froze to the iron handles of the trolleys. "There were plenty of times that the trolleys and carts, with as many as twenty banana boxes full of books and comics, would unbalance falling over into Bow Street outside the 'Knags Head' [2009, Shute Bar]."* Different generations of market traders had also used as storage space the facilities offered within the basement of the Town Hall – the Beeley's were no exception as Jason well remembered, *"The basement was quite scary for a young lad and to get the trolleys out you had to navigate a steep incline - this was very hard, for if you didn't get a good enough run up you could get halfway before you realised you weren't going to make it – then it was a matter of getting out of the way before it all rolled back and slammed you against the wall at the bottom".* Just like any schoolboy of the time there were occasions when playing truant from school became de rigueur for young Jason however, this occurred so he could help out on the family stall. *"Mum worked at Marks & Spencer's at the time and would come out at dinner time to see Dad, suddenly I'd get a shout from a trader 'your mum's on her way'. "I'd crouch down, get on my hands and knees and make my way under the other stalls until I'd get to the end and out of sight of mum. Not one of the traders would bat an eyelid at me at going under their stalls, all that was said was, 'I take it your mum's about then Jason', they would all cover for me, 'Yes he went to school again Mrs Beeley' they'd say".*

In 1981 Ashton's outdoor market began trading six days a week with Tuesdays being allocated for use as a flea market. Although only originally started for a trial period and getting off to a rather slow start the second-hand dealers soon proved there was a demand for such a market – as there still is today. The weather was bitterly cold on the Tuesday before Christmas and only half of the stalls were occupied. However, the hardy traders that had turned up all reported a good day's business. Over the first few weeks though, many traders must have wondered if it was all worthwhile, the weather was absolutely atrocious with one stall being completely blown over. Among those brave enough to ply their trade through those initial gruelling weeks were Hilda King who had cleared her shelves of kitchen utensils to sell, John Parker a dealer in government surplus stock and Derek Duckworth who sold coins and medals. Mr Parker who travelled from Cheetham Hill to attend the market did rather well selling green army jersey's – these proved to be his best sellers along with the army boots apparently worth

Ashton's Flea Market
Derek Duckworth – Coining it in?

£50 but which he sold for just £6. He also had a nice line in string vests which were snapped up for £3.50 by the local punk rockers giving Mr Parker a good £3.10 profit per item. One trader who found a place for anything and everything on his stall commented, *"It seems you have to take the rough with the smooth on a flea market".*

The organising of the Tuesday flea market would have been one of the last tasks undertaken by market manager Philip Poulter prior to his retirement. Mr Poulter had held his position for twenty-six years (1955–1981) during which he proved to be popular and well respected by everyone connected with the market. Roy Smith who worked alongside Mr Poulter for three years (1976–1979) recalled the man. *"He was arguably one of the best market managers in the north west of England at the time and was greatly respected by both traders and staff for his attention to detail and his firmness, but fairness in every aspect of retail market operations and management. "The knowledge Philip Poulter imparted and the invaluable experience gained from our working relationship was to serve me in good stead when I left Tameside to take up the different situation of 'works manager' for the larger authority which was Salford.*

Having carried out nothing much more than general maintenance works during the 1970s, it was to be 1983 before the council again was to undergo any considerable improvements to Ashton's market area. At this time Warrington Street facing Marks and Spencer's and Woolworths was pedestrianised. A number of trees were planted and flower displays adorned a walled seating area. A further three kiosks were installed in the style of those already in place. Other minor improvements along with a general tidying up of the whole area were also undertaken. It was about this time that Fred Rust retired consequently selling his roundabout which had been in the family for around forty years. With the earlier departure of the Seldon's the other long established ride proprietors an era in the market's history had now come to an end. Eventually however, the rides would once again find owners of long standing in the form of Vic Coase (ten years) and Joe Zhara (twenty-plus years).

Over the last weekend of September 1984 the council and market traders, clinging to a belief that Ashton's market charter had been granted in 1284, joined forces to celebrate what mistakenly they took to be the 700th anniversary of the granting of the market charter. On Friday evening a procession led by Ashton's legendary 'Black Knight' made it's way through the streets to the steps of the town hall. Upon their arrival the market manager Mr John Mullin acting as King Edward I and his Queen played by market stalwart 'Queenie', handed over a decorated parchment representing the charter, to Robert de Assheton who was played by Tameside's Mayor councillor Geoff Brierly. A good sized crowd was in attendance and many more were in and around the shops, which had remained open late.

Market Manager John Mullin (right), with 'Queenie' presenting 'charter' to Mayor councillor Geoff Brierly (left). Robert Sheldon MP is pictured second from left.

The market ground was still attracting the late shoppers even though many outside traders had decided against remaining. Saturday morning shoppers saw a rare sight when a town crier paraded the streets and market area announcing Saturday's programme of events. Morris dancers, Singers, Magicians, bands and other entertainers, from varying points on the market, suitably amused and delighted the public. Joining in the spirit of the occasion were members of the local 'Round Table' who organised 'Merlin's Catch'- a mouse game, a ducking stool, and a pillory. The whole area was bustling throughout the day and traders taking part entered into the spirit of the occasion. Staff on many stalls dressed-up resulting in an overabundance of Friar Tucks and Robin Hoods. Assistants from Hartley's children's wear stall were in period dress whilst those at Finnerty's cafe were dressed as serving wenches.

Medieval merriment with stall holders and the local 'Round Table' all joining in the fun of the occasion.

A packed market ground all there to see the switch on of the 1984 Christmas lights

Two years later John Finnerty died and ownership of the cafe was transferred to his wife Estella Finnerty and for a further four years she continued to run things as they had been over the years. Estella retired in 1990 when her daughter Claire took over for a short time before the business was sold to S. Williams who had the provisions stall almost opposite. The sale brought to an end what was over a seventy year association between the cafe and the Finnerty family.

1990 was also the year which saw the determination and courage of a young Ashton woman touch the hearts of everyone. Mandy Turner was just 21 years old and had been diagnosed with a rare and painful form of muscular cancer and had been given just six months to live. Because of the lack of facilities at Tameside General Hospital Mandy set out in a quest to raise one million pounds to provide the hospital with its own scanner. From the day she started the fund money began to flood in, to the extent that the target figure was reached within thirty one weeks. Sadly just nine days later Mandy lost her fight for life. Hundreds attended her funeral service at which the minister described her as a girl in a million. The scanner for which Mandy had worked so hard was opened at the hospital in October 1990. Throughout the campaign a most unusual fundraiser became a popular figure on Ashton market at the greengrocery stall of Alan and Ruth Rhodes. Sandy, the proprietors' mongrel dog dressed in a body warmer and balaclava became quite an attraction as unfazed by all the attention he would sit calmly in his basket allowing the public to pat, stroke, cuddle or shake a paw for a donation to the fund. In all kinds of weather Sandy would remain at his task charming the public and winning countless admirers many of whom would also give him little treats. At the final count Sandy and the good hearted market shoppers had raised £4,000 towards Mandy's Scanner Appeal.

Sandy helped raise £4000 on Ashton Market for the Mandy Turner Scanner Appeal

In order to keep Ashton's place as a major shopping centre in the region, the early 1990s saw the start of work which upon completion would vastly transform the whole of the town centre, taking it into the next century. Some of the work involved in this development saw lengths of Wood Street and Wellington Street between George Street and Delamere Street being pedestrianised. Following on from this, Warrington Street now became fully pedestrianised as work on the stretch from Stamford Street leading towards the market area was completed. Further streets to become traffic free were Old Street from close to the old Metro cinema up to the junction of Market Street and George Street. Turning left the work continued to include the pedestrianisation of Market Street and Bow Street. The making of these pedestrian areas didn't just mean closing streets to traffic, for they also took on a new appearance with the original footpaths and roads blending into one by the laying down of red brick. Ornamental metal posts were strategically placed along what would have been the old kerbstone edge which added to the whole new look and in some cases helped in allowing entry for service or emergency vehicles. Before work had even started on the market ground this and other completed environmental improvements made the area more attractive to shoppers.

Early in 1992 when issuing detailed plans for the market ground, the council angered the traders whose association spoke out against the proposed changes, for it would see the market being reduced in size with a loss of seventeen stalls. They saw this as being a sad loss to Ashton which would also affect the indoor market and surrounding shops. It would also result in fewer casual traders being allowed to trade, which would in turn have a long term effect on the Market's future. In an effort to try and get the council to have a rethink, traders joined together in a campaign to win the support of the public. A petition was organised, posters were displayed and adverts placed in the local press urging the public to contact their local councillor in protest. Their efforts did win over the public and a petition carrying 12,000 signatures was handed over to Mayor of Tameside councillor John Hughes, who commented that the petition was one of the biggest he'd ever seen. Having made people more aware of the situation and after putting in a lot of hard work the traders were rewarded in June with the announcement that the council had devised a new scheme. This new plan would

HELP TO SAVE ASHTON MARKET

This is an appeal to all Ashton-under-Lyne Townsfolk and others who love Ashton Market. The Market is to be made smaller, in area, as well as a loss of stalls.

It may well look pretty but it will be a sad loss to Ashton, affecting the indoor Market and the surrounding shops.

Please, please help, by cutting out the adjacent form and sending it to your local councillor, care of the Town Hall, or take it with you when you pay your rent or Poll Tax.

ST. MICHAEL'S WARD
William Wilkinson 212 Whiteacre Road Ashton-u-Lyne OL6 9PZ
Lena Easton 23 Cumberland Grove Ashton-u-Lyne OL7 9BS
Marjorie Bennett 137 Rosehill Road Ashton-under-Lyne OL6 8HR

ST. PETERS WARD
Terry Kenyon 8 Higham Lane Gee Cross, Hyde SK14 5LX
Andrew Cassidy 18 Anglesey Close Ashton-under-Lyne OL7 9NJ
Warren Bray "Ring-o-Bells" 151 Margaret Street Ashton-under-Lyne OL6 7TS

WATERLOO WARD
Brian Lees 135 Taunton Road Ashton-under-Lyne
Catherine Piddington 157 Oldham Road Ashton-under-Lyne OL7 9AR
Robert Parker 1 Sunnyside Off Newmarket Road Ashton-under-Lyne

HURST WARD
M. M. Foote 32 Glendon Crescent Ashton-under-Lyne
Alan Whitehead 2 Springbank Avenue Ashton-under-Lyne OL6 8QL
Peter Joinson Handforth Cottage Gambrel Bank Ashton-under-Lyne OL6 8TJ

To Councillor ....
From ....
Address ....
I object to any alterations to my Market that results in it being made smaller in any way.
Signature ....

1992 – Petition posters & leaflets circulated the town and appeared in the local press

The times they are a changing...

...The same scene taken thirty years apart

Top: ***1960s Market Street populated with several motor vehicles***

Bottom: ***1990s after pedestrianisation***

now only result in five stalls being lost as opposed to the original seventeen, and according to the council, the market sales area would actually be 2% bigger than envisaged. Committee chairman councillor Jim Fitzpatrick said; *this scheme will be a great improvement on the present market". "It will be a cleaner safer market providing a more attractive environment and a customer friendly area in which to shop".* It was expected that the work involved would take around six months to complete, therefore a temporary site, enabling the market to continue trading during this period was required. In an attempt to re-site the stalls as near as possible to the market hall and main shopping area, the car park between Fletcher Street and Old Cross Street was designated as a temporary market site, along with a position at the corner of Fletcher Street and Market Street and indeed some stalls, mainly greengrocers, were to be situated on the recently pedestrianised Market Street close to the Market Hall. The task of removing the stalls from the market ground to their temporary home was started on Saturday January 6th 1993 at 6pm after close of the days trading, and work was completed by lunch time on Sunday.

The task of removing stalls from the market ground commenced at 6pm on Saturday January 6th. With the work being completed by lunch time on Sunday

Having encountered very few difficulties in setting up the new site, Ashton's temporary market ground opened to the public on the morning of Monday January 11th. Within days the old market ground had been fenced off in readiness for the contractors to commence work. Notices pointing the public towards the direction of the temporary market were posted near to the bus station and around the central shopping area, whilst details were published in the local press. The total costs involved in refurbishing Ashton's historic market amounted to £1.3million; however £500,000 of this had been received from a European regional development grant.

As the original market ground is turned into a building site...

... shoppers buy their goods from the temporary location

It wasn't long before the town centre took on a new face as work commenced. Wythenshaw paving contractors P.P. Doherty were the ones who had responsibility for the resurfacing of the whole market area. One hundred and fifty-one new stalls were constructed by Denton's Beresford Building Contractors and with seven large domed kiosks the market began to take shape. External cold water mains were installed along with a new drainage system by Portland Associates of Bolton. Councillor Cath Piddington chairman of Tameside's Market panel had explained why this refurbishment had to be carried out: *"Ashton's market has been an important commercial centre for many centuries. It is important that the market can compete with developments in other towns in the area. The new market will prove to be a catalyst for drawing new shoppers into the town".* While the traders agreed with these sentiments they were far from happy with the situation they found themselves in because of the upheaval. During the first few weeks of trading on their temporary site a good many were slating the move saying that it was a disaster for them. They spoke of reluctance among the public to walk to this new site and of how many of them may be forced into ceasing trading. For a time it seemed that many traders did indeed suffer, however, business did pick up somewhat following an improvement in the weather and an increase of stalls along Market Street. As April approached several stallholders were expressing a desire that those stalls which had been relocated to Market Street for the duration of the improvement work should remain there after the work was completed. A number of shop proprietors on Market Street also backed this move stating that the stalls had brought the street to life.

With everything seemingly progressing well and the new market ground set for completion on time further echoes of discontent came from a section of the market traders. These were now voicing their objections to a number of points concerning the, as yet unfinished market area. No matter what their opinions were however, the council, with just over a month left for the hand-over day of Monday 28th June, found themselves with a big demand for stalls. With Tuesday now well established as the day for the Flea Market it was decided that Wednesday June 30th should be the first day of trading, with an official opening to take place on Saturday July 3rd. Chairman of the town's Chamber of Trade Mr Raymond Blain said; *"the reopening of the market will give a massive boost to the town. "This will be very, very welcome following the long and difficult recession. All of the town's traders will be joining forces with the council to make the day a great success".* It was thought that the use of a celebrity for the reopening would help in rejuvenating Ashton and in bringing back more customers. However, the announcement that televisions 'Coronation Street' actor Ken Morley, alias 'Randy' Reg Holdsworth was to receive an impressive £1,500 for conducting the opening ceremony caused a storm of

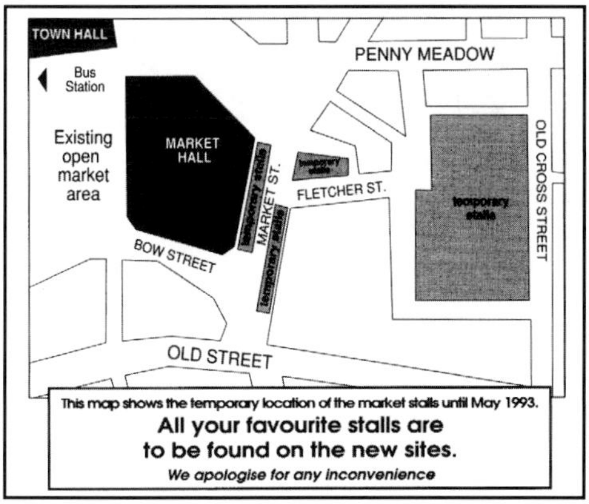

Part of a leaflet showing the location of the temporary site

protest amongst the public. Numerous letters were received by the local newspapers all of which expressed outrage at the council for wasting this kind of money; the writers felt that the Mayor could perform the honours equally as well and at a fraction of the cost. It wasn't until after the market had been officially reopened that the truth came out, when the council's publicity spokesman Sean Harris revealed; the bill for actor Ken Morley had not solely been met by the council. Apparently many local traders had donated money themselves towards the reopening and this had contributed to the star's fee. If this information had been made clear before the opening of the market a number of people would not have reacted in the way that they did to the news about the hiring of a celebrity.

A poster announcing the 1993 market 'grand re-opening' by actor Ken Morley

The morning of Saturday July 3rd 1993 had seen the traders arriving at the market early, perhaps with eager anticipation of a good day's trading. The public, many of whom were making their first visit to the revamped site gradually followed, and by 9.30am the area was amass with people. Mingling within the hordes of shoppers browsing around the well stacked stalls were a number of entertainers engaged by the council to give the occasion a fun element, a day for the whole family to enjoy. Ronald McDonald, the burger restaurant clown, was strolling around like a pied-piper leading children in the direction of his eatery. Whilst other children and their parents stood watching as a stilt walker passed them by. Music from a disco, provided by the hospital radio service, 'Eight Towns Radio' filled the air, as too did the sounds of a 'Dixieland Jazz Band'. It had been said that the numbers on the market that morning were in excess of 4,000.

Part of the 4,000 strong crowd who had gathered for the official reopening of the Market by actor Ken Morley

At around 10am a good many of these were still surrounding the stalls while others numbering about 2,000 gathered in the new civic square, the paved area, fronting the town hall eagerly awaiting the arrival of Ken Morley. Local DJ and actor Simon Frater, whose job it was to entertain the public prior to Mr Morley's arrival, soon had the public on his side and a good many in the crowd hardly noticed that the 'soap' star was late in arriving. Although the official time for the opening was to be 11am, it was to be over 30 minutes later before Mr Morley made his belated appearance. The Mayor Councillor Albert Hatton eventually getting the proceedings under way introduced Councillor Cath Piddington the chairman of the markets sub-committee, who in turn gave thanks to all those involved with the work which had been carried out adding; *"Ashton market is now the best in the north west".* At this point it was the turn of the person for whom almost everyone present had turned out to see, after being delayed as a result of his car breaking down on route to town Ken Morley entered onto the town hall steps. Sporting a vivid yellow jacket he immediately drew bouts of laughter from a string of one-liners delivered with all the style of a seasoned entertainer. Following a short speech Mr Morley and Councillor Piddington together unveiled a commemorative plaque whilst at the same time declaring the market open. During the festivities 709 balloons were launched towards the sky, one for every year of the town's market charter, as the market committee would have you believe that is, for they will not agree with modern historians regarding actual date. The day continued with thousands of people enjoying their shopping amidst a varied sound of music and laughter until late in the afternoon.

Left*: Ken Morley entertains the thronged market place.*
Right*: 709 balloons are released*

For several months after the opening of the revamped market ground there were still a number of complaints being aired by one or two stallholders and members of the public. Most of these amounted to nothing more than teething troubles and the reaction by some people to their dislike of change.

The 'new look' market ground - 1993

Several noticeable transformations within the market hall were shortly to take place. The closure of Bailey's hardware came as a surprise to many people, as it had been a name associated with the market for over 140 years. However, in this case all was not as it appeared, for Mr Gary Buckley, the proprietor of Bailey's Hardware and the nearby Bailey's Electrical had, since acquiring these businesses in 1980 been locked in a fierce rivalry with Mr Cyril Berkman the owner of Moss' Hardware and

Moss' Electrical. After Mr Berkman retired, Gary Buckley managed to obtain his businesses. However, with only being allowed by market rules to own three stalls he sold Bailey's Hardware transferring all of its trade to the newly acquired Moss' stall. The Bailey name continued to be associated with the hall by way of the remaining Electrical stall. Various other retailers at this period also moved on or relocated. Lamentably, no longer did the market hall boast a 'Queenie's' stall. Filling the gaps vacated by these 'older' names and ensuring that the market stalls remained occupied were a fresh group of traders. Where once upon a time it was possible to have seen 'Valvona' wafers or examined 'Butterick' sewing patterns, instead 'Nike' and 'Reebock' sports and casual wear could be discovered. It was now possible to buy a greetings card or wrapping paper from where once a pork pie or a pound of tripe could have been purchased. Stalls belonging to Dando's (Watches) and the grocery business of Redman's situated against the Market Street wall were both taken over to trade in different lines - The latter being acquired by Jason Beeley a trader who had worked the outdoor market selling books and stationery since 1983. Then as a fifteen-year-old he was venturing into business in his own right having previously helped on the family stall since 1977. He began trading in new books his initial stock bought with the £300 capital given to him by his parents. Although acquiring the old Redman's stall Jason continued to stand the open market but with a change of direction, the books and stationery were transferred to the indoor market making way for the new lines of picture frames and pictures. Nicola, soon to become Jason's wife, ran the indoor stall with the occasional help from Jason's relatives and the business

Beeley's books and stationery business transferred from the market ground to the indoor market and occupied the old Redman's stall.

operated successfully becoming quite a popular stall. On the outside however, Jason's new venture had really taken off and with the extra time needed to set out his display he was finding it more difficult – it would often take up to three hours to set up his stall. Therefore, after five years of trading in the market hall it was decided to relinquish the stall freeing-up the extra help Jason needed. As always the march of time saw market traders suitably adjusting to modern trends by presenting to the people their current needs. At the time that Beeley and others were adjusting to life in the indoor market those outside stalls retailing in greengroceries had diminished and in their stead came stalls dealing in confectionary, household goods and fresh fish. This latter stall, belonging to Crossley's caught the attention of the public during April 1994 when they had on view a six foot 23-stone shark The shark, the largest to be caught that year off the coast of Cornwall, had cost Mark Crossley the princely sum of £500. The large fish was eventually cut up and distributed throughout their other shops in the Manchester area.

1994 was also the year which saw a major change in people's shopping habits. This came about with the relaxation of the Sunday trading laws. Prior to this a number of small shops had opened, but from Sunday August 29th in most towns and cities throughout the country Sundays would never be the same. For on this day the big major high street shops and out of town supermarkets began seven day trading which made an impact everywhere. Initially Ashton's town centre saw little change with only a handful of shops opening for business. It was not until 1995 and the opening of the Arcades Shopping Centre that Sundays in town became busier. However, although Sunday shoppers in town were increasing Ashton Market remained closed.

Since the Market refurbishment of 1993 some traders had been allowed to pitch stalls on Bow Street, Market Street and Warrington Street facing the Marks & Spencer's store. By 1996 however, fresh initiatives were introduced by new market's manager Ian Kelly which included the reintroduction of the showman type of trader - a throwback to a tradition of old. Most of these retailers were those who used temporary pitches or utilised their own motor vehicles – further echoes of the past. With the passing of time however, these showmen type vendors ceased being 'showmen' becoming instead merely like any other stall holder. One of the most popular of the new traders introduced in 1996 was the butcher who sold his meat from a vehicle at the corner of Bow Street and Market Street. Initially, many butchers from the market hall objected to this practice, and one nearby shop closed soon after his arrival. However, the mobile-butcher vehicle soon became popular and one still stood a similar position in 2009.

Although many businesses both at the outdoor and indoor markets had their regular customers there can not have been many stalls like 'Hats and Things' which attracted clientele from far and wide. 'Hats and Things' traded from within one of the market hall shop units situated to the left of the corner

Bow Street/Market Ground entrance. People regularly made the journey from such places as Blackpool, Yorkshire and London to buy from the little shop; the reason being the reputation of Harriet Clegg – known to everyone as 'Hattie Harriet'. The hats she sold were of the highest quality and would not have been out of place in London's Regent Street. Although Harriet ran the business it was actually owned by her daughter Maureen Wallis whose only real involvement was to drive Harriet to Manchester and beyond to buy hats.

Harriet Clegg.
Known to everyone as 'Hattie Harriet' she attracted clientele from far and wide to 'Hats and Things'

Though never having received any formal training Harriet had a natural talent for design, an eye for detail, a flair for colour and she knew her hats – attributes which gained her prominence. In 1997 Maureen decided to pursue other interests and was also thinking that Harriet, who had just celebrated her 70th birthday, was working to hard and should be taking things easy, although Harriet herself disagreed. With this in mind Maureen made the decision to cease trading. However, it was not to be the end for 'Hattie Harriet' as Christine Makin the new proprietor wanted to be just that 'the proprietor'. Therefore Harriet was asked to remain in exclusive control of everything from managing the unit to purchasing the stock. *"I first started working in the market when my nephew Clifford Wildgoose, who then ran a coat stall, asked me to help him. From the start I loved it especially with 'Hats and Things' which had such a good reputation".* Harriet smiled broadly as she recalled the visit of one lady to the shop. She entered carrying a dress over one arm – a black dress with big bold blue flowers printed on to it. She was seeking a hat in the same shade of blue, informing Harriet that she had seen something similar in the window. After trying on the hat the woman exclaimed 'That's it! You wouldn't believe the trouble I've had finding this'. 'You like it then, do you?' asked Harriet. 'Well

I think it looks awful on you, it's the wrong colour and it's not even the right size'. Although the woman insisted it was right Harriet managed to persuade her into allowing five minutes in which to show her something else. During this time she took a black hat on which she placed seven little blue flowers. On trying on the hat the woman proclaimed 'It's amazing, you are marvellous, and I've been everywhere, across Lancashire, Cheshire and Manchester and who would have thought I'd get fixed up in a market'. But of course that's the beauty of Ashton Market and people, like Harriet.

Town centre Ashton had since the introduction of the Sunday trading laws become increasingly busier. However, it was not until 1998 that the market ground was to open for Sunday trading. Again, this was to be a throwback to what Ashton's very first market would have been like as the townspeople were invited to come along to sell their surplus goods. At this time car boot sales and table top sales had become a popular Sunday pastime for many people. Following these lines the market began to hold a weekly giant table top sale – initially for a trial during the summer months. Although not blessed with much decent weather the potential for such a market must have been noted as the following year this Sunday market returned and remains popular today.

Chapter Six.

To market, Jenny come trot,
Spilt all her butter-milk, every drop.
Every drop and every dram,
Jenny came home with an empty can

A modern Ashton Market Hall with Turkish cannon in foreground

The change in retailing during the second half of the 20th century was particularly dramatic. Traditional high street shopping habits had now totally altered. The spread of '24 hour' supermarkets, the large out of town shopping malls and the growth of personal transport had all contributed to this major revolution.

Entering the 21st century and due in no small part to new technology a new form of retailing quickly emerged in the form of Internet trading. All in all this created new challenges for local shops and traditional markets such as those in Ashton.

Ashton Market has always occupied an important place in the day to day life of society and has provided a focal point for the local community even when faced with such formidable competition. Entering the new millennium the market still maintained its status as a major shopping attraction.

In April 2000 the council announced plans that would see a change of use, once a month for the open market ground. It was their intention to establish a Farmers and Craft Market to operate on the last Sunday of every month. This would mean the now popular 'table top sale' would be greatly reduced on these Sundays to allow room for the new traders. The Farmers' Market was an idea imported from America and was introduced to Britain in Bath during August 1997. Since then their popularity in various towns gained momentum something which had been noticed by Tameside Council and for twelve months they made their plans to launch a similar one in Ashton.

The whole concept of Farmers' Markets was really nothing new to Ashton being more akin to the original and traditional market of yesteryear. Today a Farmers' Market is a place where farmers' and producers from a local area sell their own produce. At Ashton all non-foods items must have been produced within 30 miles of the market, while with foodstuffs a limit of 50 miles put a guarantee on their freshness - with everything on offer being traceable. Some vegetables for example may have only been taken from the ground the night before they were put up for sale – not many shops could boast that. In addition because the food and goods available had not travelled great distances customers had the satisfaction of knowing they had helped to reduce the environmental impact of transportation.

Announcing the start of Ashton's Farmers' Market April 2000 – And still going strong

Ashton's first Farmers' Market took place on Sunday 30th April 2000 and all expectations were surpassed. It was estimated that between 8,000 and 10,000 people packed the market ground that day and so successful was it that most of the forty-five traders had sold their stock before lunch time. During its first year the popularity of the Farmers' Market increased and in December of 2001 the market was in the running for a national prize after picking up the regional National Farmers Union 'Best Farmers' Market Award'. Ian Kelly market's manager put the success down to a lot of hard work and a fantastic choice of products. The market had grown to become the biggest in the North West offering a wide range of food producers and around 35 to 40 craft stalls. The first person to be granted one of the craft stalls was local artist Arthur Broadhead, who soon became a popular character. From his stall Arthur would sell art prints along with original pieces. He became a familiar sight sitting at his easel sketching the

Artist Arthur Broadhead Christened his stall 'Pill Corner'.

shoppers as they mingled amongst the stalls. Situated at the corner near to the town hall and Wellington Road, Arthur's pitch soon earned the nickname of pill corner. Arthur's wife, Pat explained, *"This was something Arthur affectionately Christened it, as many of our regular visitors were the elderly or infirm – many just wanted to talk nostalgically while others chatted about their complaints and illnesses – but Arthur listened to them all".* Since being a young lad Arthur had always had a love affair with Ashton's market and was well known to many traders in the Market Hall for his sign writing skills – with his work adorning many of their stalls.

From that beginning Ashton's Farmers' Market grew in stature and is still a regular monthly event today [2009] when there can be seen as many as sixty food stalls and a dozen craft stalls offering their wares. Still operating alongside this is what the council continues to officially call a 'Table Top Sale' – yet in recent years it appears to have become much more than that.

As part of the Borough's Commonwealth Games celebrations a real flavour of the continent engulfed the market area over the weekend of July 26th-28th 2002. Over thirty European traders had set up their stalls along Bow Street, Market Street and Fletcher Sq near to the Family Sculpture, in what was the town's first ever Continental Market. The event organised by 'Market Initiatives Ltd' attracted thousands of visitors over the three day period especially on the Sunday when the popular Farmers' Market also took place. Today in various parts of the country Continental Markets are often quite an attraction especially at Christmas time; however for the

One French stall holder offers a variety of Fougasse (bread) flavoured with strong herbs, or stuffed with cheese, bacon, butter, or olives.

people of Ashton during the summer of 2002 it was a totally new experience. Belgian chocolate, cider and champagne from France, meat from Corsica, Bread from Brittany, Italian food products and leather goods and a range of German beers were all amongst a variety of items for sale. One stall which proved to be hugely popular was that of Dick Van De Wardt known as 'The Flying Dutchman' whose array of plants, shrubs and bulbs were eagerly snapped up. The market certainly created a different atmosphere and in hearing many foreign accents and taking in the various aromas you could almost believe you were abroad.

A touch of mainland Europe comes to Ashton with a Continental Market. 'The Flying Dutchman' presented an assortment of plants, shrubs and bulbs which were all eagerly snapped up.

By 2004 Ashton's major stores along with the Arcades and Ladysmith Shopping Centres were helping maintain the town's reputation as one of the regions top town centres. Both the indoor and outdoor markets were still attracting people from far and wide and were recognised as the one of the best around. Further accolade was to be bestowed when in February 2004 the monthly Farmers' Market was acknowledged by the Observer Food Magazine as being number one in the North West.

Since the market moved to its present site in 1830 there have been many notable dates in its history, none more so than Tuesday May 24th 2004. This was the date that disaster struck in the early hours of the morning. At around 3.00am the fire service based in Stalybridge received a call activated by the alarm system installed within Ashton's market hall. Acting swiftly they arrived in Ashton to be greeted by flames and smoke billowing from the roof of the grade II listed building. The magnitude of the blaze resulted in crews from all over Greater Manchester being called upon as Ashton's brigade was at the time suspended due to an industrial dispute. At the peak of the conflagration a ninety strong force was in attendance with Bow Street, Market Street, Wellington Road and the market ground being lined with a total of nineteen tenders many of which carried specialist equipment in order to quell the raging fire. Spreading at an alarming rate flames shot even higher into the smoke filled air as the clock tower became engulfed. With the whole roof destroyed the interior of the hall was one massive fireball contained only by the outer walls – these being the only remains once the fire had died.

The market clock tower engulfed in flames

There was a strong feeling of disbelief amongst the crowds which soon began to gather around the market area. A crowd increasing in numbers as the local radio stations broke the news and the time moved towards the morning rush hour. As we made the journey into town we seemed to be in a stream of people all heading for the same destination. Upon our arrival we were greeted by a scene which we can only describe as eerie. For a moment we stood in a state of shock as not for one second did we expect to see what was now before us.

Left: ***The raging Inferno pictured from Market Street.***

Centre: The devastation captured from the Town Hall roof.

Bottom: ***Daylight and water is still being pumped into the remains of the building.***

In a few short hours over 174 years of history had literally gone up in smoke, taking with it the livelihoods of many traders. The market hall along with the outdoor market was the heart of the community, it had been a way of life for generations of people who shopped and socialised there. Now it was just a smouldering pile of ash and rubble.

Although the crowds had increased in numbers since our arrival, strangely everyone seemed motionless except for the many reporters from the press, TV and radio who were anxiously seeking out stall holders or anyone who had a comment to make on the tragic event. Suddenly we were confronted by a reporter from GMR (Radio Manchester) who had been trying to contact us since early morning. After the briefest of introductions a microphone was thrust before us and within a couple of minutes our thoughts were history and the reporter had moved on just as quickly as he had arrived. We saw the distraught figure of butcher David Conn, who had spent a lifetime in the market hall, but before we could reach him a reporter from the press intervened. Emotionally David explained to him how he had worked in the market since being 15 years of age, he was now 87. He went on to say how he had hoped to complete three quarters of a century and how he had served daughters of daughters, each word spoken with a nervous sincerity. As the reporter departed a clearly upset David also moved away – we left him to his grief. A stallholder from the Sunday craft market and a well known character, artist Arthur Broadhead was also visibly distraught when interviewed for a regional television news bulletin. *"I'm absolutely devastated, I just can't.... This is all about.... This is the finest market in the country and the finest people in the world and I'm absolutely.... and I feel like breaking down, it's awful",* said Arthur, which just about echoed the thoughts of everyone. Harriet Clegg who ran 'Hats and Things' said, *"Although normally closed on Tuesdays I had intended to open up in order to take a delivery of hats. "These were quite expensive and really good quality all individually made, from Whiteley's the country's leading hat manufacturers. "The order was for around £2,000 and but for a delay would have been delivered on the Monday and gone up in smoke".* As Harriet was about to leave home for the market on the Tuesday morning she took a phone call informing her of the fire, *"I was speechless, it was so sad, such a loss for everyone".*

David Conn just a few years earlier in happier times.

The aftermath of the fire saw several businesses on Market Street and Bow Street being forced into temporary closure due to health and safety concerns. A number of market traders were also affected as stalls were removed from the market ground to enable the clear up to begin. After the dampening down operation had been completed the whole perimeter of the hall was fenced off with temporary scaffolding being erected to shore up the damaged sections of the walls. This enabled the safety of the remaining market structure to be checked and allowed fire investigators to enter the site. Working alongside the police and forensic science service they were faced with a massive task of sifting through the remains of 116 burnt out stalls in an effort to discover the root of the fire.

Within two days of the fire, market staff announced that the market ground would be open for business on Saturday although stalls would be restricted to half the usual number. The monthly Farmers' Market due the following day (Sunday) was also given the go-ahead. This news, added to the fact that the annual Black Knight Pageant was taking place that same weekend, which also included a fun fair on the Old Cross Street car park, resulted in a bustling town centre.

Tameside council were also quick to reassure the traders' whose livelihoods had been lost that everything possible would be done to help rectify the situation. It was stated that steps had been taken to identify a site for a temporary market hall. Councillor Kieran Quinn however, said that this may take some time, adding, *"we're doing all we can to open an indoor market as quickly as possible, but I don't want to give any false impressions or raise peoples expectations too soon."*

In conjunction with the two local newspapers the Council launched the 'Ashton Market Hall Phoenix Fund. The aim of which was to raise one million pounds to provide 'seed corn' funding for those traders not insured against the fire enabling them to acquire sufficient stock to restart their business within the temporary market hall. Unfortunately many of the townsfolk picked up on the wrong idea of the fund and mistakenly thought that its motive was to finance the recreation of the Market. The Phoenix Fund was completely independently run and wholly separate from Tameside Council, with its trustees, including David Heyes MP, ensuring the highest levels of probity in the conduct of the fund and its eventual disbursements.

The council were rather limited in their choices of a suitable site to house a temporary market hall especially within the bounds of the town centre. They eventually chose the Old Cross Street car park which over the years had been used for many different events and also staged the outdoor market in 1993. The new building was to be a 2400 sq metre modular construction and was chosen from seven different types of modular buildings and would consist of three halls, one food and two for non-food.

Work soon began on the foundations and the prefabricated structure arrived in sections over a three week period from a Hull based company Marchant Walker.

Work on constructing the 'Phoenix Market' moved at a rapid pace

The old market building had by now been declared unsafe and with public safety in mind the temporary scaffolding was dismantled and replaced by a more permanent structure which surrounded the whole building. Once the outer walls had been securely supported contractors moved in to tackle the huge job of removing the debris from within the perimeter walls. At this point the team of investigators were vacating the site, they had a good idea of when the fire had started but it was very difficult for them to establish the cause. Divisional fire officer Barry Jones said, *"I have never done a fire investigation like this in my life it's like looking for a needle in a haystack".* The investigators were looking for evidence which due to the magnitude of the fire – it even melted cast iron – was difficult to find. It soon became clear that their resources could not be maintained and in a later report they stated that the source of the fire would never be known, the most that could be said was that it was probably caused by an appliance or the mains electricity within the building. There was also a possibility that small amounts of asbestos would be found in the rubble so all appropriate precautions were put into place. The Health and Safety Executive was called in to develop safe methods of work and to advise on the safe removal of the debris.

The kiosks directly in front of the market hall, although not damaged by the fire, were forced to close due to the fencing in of the building and were eventually demolished. Kim Wright lost her ice cream kiosk but trade in these lines was transferred to her 'Mr Spuds' kiosk on the opposite side of the market, close to the children's roundabouts. Since acquiring 'Mr Spuds' in 1995 Kim would often say to Joe Zharah the owner of the roundabouts, how she would like to purchase the rides on his retirement. The rides held a special interest for Kim as they were once owned by her great aunt, Nora Rust. As a child Kim would often accompany her grandmother to the market and a visit to Aunt Nora and a ride on the roundabout was always a treat to look forward to. So when Joe eventually retired in 2004 after twenty years with the rides, it was perhaps fitting that they should have returned to Kim's family. Soon after making the purchase Kim discovered a few Health and Safety concerns. However, as the rides were so old it was difficult to source any required spare parts. Kim and her husband, realising that this was a major problem which would become worse with time decided to replace one ride with a brand new state of the art carousel. After a trip to Bursa in Turkey they found a manufacturer which built rides for theme parks and an order was made. The new carousel would take a good few months to be built and shipped over to Britain and would not open until January 2005.

Temporary fencing hid the kiosks which due to their close proximity to the market were eventually demolished.

By September 2004 the temporary hall had been completed and a total of sixty-one traders had agreed to be relocated. Those that declined the opportunity were given the same assurances as the continuing market traders that everyone would be allowed into the new hall upon completion of its rebuild. Those dealing in foodstuffs were the first to be allowed into the new Phoenix Market giving them chance to install any of their bulky or specialist equipment. A short time later and all other traders began to prepare their stalls for the grand opening on 15th October. When the temporary market opened its doors to the public 107 stalls were occupied. Some of the tenants however, were far from happy. The reason behind this was that the expected 'seed corn funding' from the publicly donated 'Phoenix Fund' in many instances had yet to be received. Initially, the 'fund' had been set up to help traders replace stock and to re-start their businesses after the fire, and although the Phoenix Hall was now open quite a few traders had still not received any financial aid. Several people were annoyed that assistance was not forthcoming quickly enough and that it had to be applied for through 'form filling'. Trader, Sid Williams said, *"You had to apply for a payment, but as we had been covered by our insurance – though not fully – we didn't actually apply, we thought we would leave it for those people in greater need".* Eventually, funding of varied amounts was distributed to the successful applicants. However, perhaps the strongest feeling of annoyance from the market traders came from the fact that amounts from the 'seed corn' funding had been received by taxi drivers who had allegedly lost trade with the closure of the market.

As the public, in their hundreds began to arrive on the opening day, all traders were at least happy at being back in business. *"The fire was devastating for many people, but that's in the past".* said Councillor Quinn, *"We now have a new market hall for shoppers and a tremendous town centre, one of the top three in the region. So we hope people join us for the opening and celebrate".*

A number of special attractions were arranged for the month of October all centred around the grand opening of the new hall on Friday 15th. Friday October 1st saw local DJ Eddie Allen entertaining the crowds around the Family Statue on Market Street adjacent to Fletcher Street. On the Saturday the road-show from local radio station Revolution moved in while the following Saturday it was live mayhem when the Flaming Nutters took to the stage. Following the official opening of the new Phoenix Market Hall on the 15th the popular three day Continental Market returned on Friday Oct 22nd-24th. The month was rounded off on Sunday 31st by what was described as the biggest and best Farmers' and Producers market in North West.

Prior to the Phoenix Market Hall opening the local press had run a competition to find a special member of the public to make the official opening. The winner chosen from the public nominations was eighty year old former market hall worker Elsie Houlton. From being a fourteen year old in 1938 Elsie had worked in the market until retiring aged 65. Among the others chosen from the competition were Alex Williams aged 11 who had battled against meningitis and Mr and Mrs Chadwick volunteers at Willow Wood Hospice. At 11.30 am on Friday 15th the Ideal New Orleans Parade Band concluded a march around the open market by stopping at the Town Hall steps. At this point the Mayor and Mayoress Councillors William and Pauline Harrison, Councillor Kieran Quinn, Ashton MP David Hayes, followed Elsie Houlton and the band in making their way to the New Market. After the formal introductions Elsie Houlton unveiled a special plaque commemorating the event to the delight of the hundreds of people who had gathered eagerly awaiting the opening of the hall. A framed picture 'The Lonely Tower' an ink sketch by Arthur Broadhead was presented

VIP Elsie Houlton officially opens the Phoenix Market accompanied by Tameside Mayor William Harrison

to the market management by Steve Bell of Peak Close Protection. The work of art which depicts the remains of the market hall after the ravages of the fire had been on display at the Central Art Gallery in Ashton. Artist and craft stall regular Arthur had donated the work to be auctioned with the proceeds going towards the Phoenix Fund. Steve Bell from the security firm of Peak Close Protection was the lucky winner and immediately thought the picture should be displayed within the Phoenix Market. Within minutes of a ribbon being cut and the hall officially declared open huge crowds descended on the stalls. Outside the entertainment continued with music coming from the Ideal New Orleans band and the Ruff Riders a Jamaican Steel Band. Throughout the weekend

The main Entrance to the temporary Phoenix Market on Swan Street

music continued to fill the air around Market Street and Fletcher Street with performances from another steel band the Pantonic All Stars and the local Carrbrook Brass Band.

All seemed to be well for the traders as the public in their thousands made their way to the new market hall. Over the first couple of weeks over 30,000 people passed through its doors, this figure had dropped to around 20,000 in late November but according to Councillor Quinn this figure was more than what had been anticipated.

In April 2005 as architects were drawing up their final design plans for the rebuilding of the Market Hall artists John Kimpton and Mac1 were about to introduce designs of their own. The pair had been sponsored by local newspaper 'The Tameside Advertiser' to illustrate the wooden hoarding surrounding the perimeter of the burnt-out listed building. Their work featured shoppers and actual market hall traders along with poems written by members of the public chosen from a competition run by the newspaper. An example of which is the following, *Ashton Market, once supreme/Since bygone times a shopper's dream/Soon it will again stand proud, attracting folk from miles around* (Ron Newman). Mac1's distinctive and highly detailed work was achieved by use of the spray can which has become his trademark. Stalybridge artist John Kimpton had also had several books published one being *'The Art of the Community'* which featured over one hundred drawings of shoppers which had been sketched during John's many visits to Ashton Market. His finished art work on the market hoardings gave the impression of shoppers in procession heading towards the Phoenix Hall; this coupled with large painted arrows was clearly an attempt at enticing the public towards temporary market.

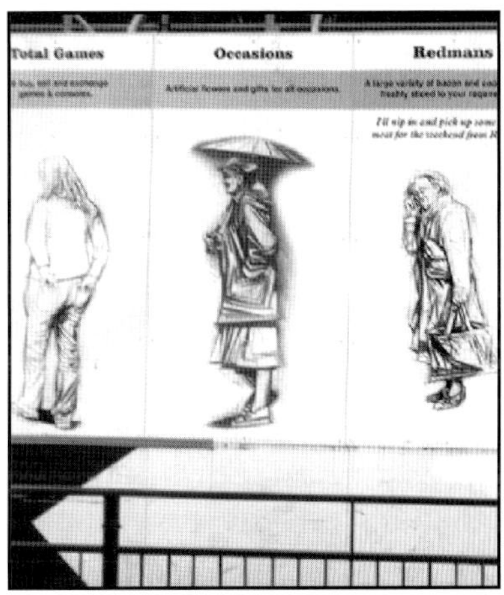

A section of hoarding showing John Kimpton's art work. A large arrow also points the way to the Phoenix Market

Although the initial concept for the new market area was to be devised by architects Patel Taylor, for a more detailed scheme the council also brought in another firm of architects Taylor Young. With plans being completed in July a number of market traders and local businesses were invited to view them before they were placed on public show. A consultation exhibition was arranged for the weekend of July 15th-17th which was held in a marquee on the market ground and attended by over 4,000 people. A questionnaire regarding the project was handed to those in attendance with over 830 being completed and returned. Comments from these were to be taken into account before any planning process began. After the event the council stated that overall local people had showed their approval of the designs, visitors to the exhibition had liked the modern feel to proposals combined with the best of the old. With the shell of the original building intact the new concept would build on the heritage features.

In the meantime the outdoor market was still attempting to attract visitors and the weekend of September 23rd–25th saw a return of the continental style market which had proved so successful in October 2004 and again in April and July this year. Sunday 25th not only saw stalls selling products from various foreign countries, but as the day also hosted the monthly farmers' market there were also traders and goods from around the region. Although not known at the time the market that Sunday would have been one of the last attended by Artist Arthur Broadhead, for little over a month later on November 1st the well known and much loved local character suffered a fatal heart attack. For sometime after his death his wife, Pat continued to run the stall until finally making the decision to give it up.

By mid-2006 the ambitious plans to redevelop the market hall had moved a step closer when government gave them their final seal of approval. Although Tameside's Speakers Panel had approved the plans earlier in the year, it had been necessary to obtain listed building consent, now finally issued. It was also announced that the main contractor for the project would be Laing O'Rourke.

Laing O'Rourke's Fletcher Street office with window illustration of 'new' market

Since the opening of Kim Wright's new carousel in January 2006 its popularity with the children had increased. However, Kim still had a decision to make regarding the other ride which was continuing to break down. Before arriving at a decision a simulator attraction was brought in and placed adjacent to the two rides. The simulator which previously had been in attendance at shows and fairs around the country proved a great success – even so, Kim made the decision to invest in another ride. Wanting something a little different than the existing carousel Kim and her husband installed a convoy ride from Italy. The surround and roof for the ride were however built in Britain to match the carousel. Speaking with Kim she talked about the rides and how she hoped they would remain on the market for many years to come. Kim also said how she had many regulars, not only children but parents and grandparents who loved to share stories

Kim Wright's new 'Kiddies Carousel' first opened on January 8th 2005

and happy memories of their childhood and the roundabouts. Kim has a sense of great pride in the fact that she is carrying on a business which was part of her family so long ago. She added, *When I go shopping in Ashton, along with my helper Lynda I feel like a bit of a celebrity when I hear children telling their parents 'look that's the roundabout lady'".*

2007 was only a few days old when the council announced that work would begin on the new market hall around the middle of January. This decision was made after they had received a £9.5million insurance payment. This money now saw all the funding for the new building finally in place – with the balance coming from the council and the Regional Development Fund. When the project did get underway the original plans had been revised with the main changes being a modification to the design of the roof due to increased costs of steel.

For some time the council had been aware that nationally traditional markets were in a state of decline and with no indications as to what the future would hold they had made specific demands to the architects. Their brief was that the new building needed to be 'future proof' while still providing a design appropriate to the market context and had to be sustainable for many years to come. Should the market ever fail, the building needed to be suitable for a wider range of potential uses such as other retail or leisure facilities or even office space. With this in mind the new roof structure was designed to minimise the number of columns within the retail floor space giving an opportunity to transform the area into smaller sections should a future need ever arise. The plans were also to include a mezzanine floor to accommodate several enterprise units to provide space for new businesses starting up in the locality. As well as the

Work underway – various shots of the market rebuilding

smaller units a larger meeting room was also to be constructed which besides being available for businesses could also be used for group or school visits.

Although building work had started it was to be sometime before the general public would actually see any real signs of progress. This and the fact that the site had been fenced off for so long led to such comments as, 'What are they doing in there?' and 'They're taking their time'. We ourselves often heard such remarks as we conversed with both traders and public and tried to explain the situation to them. In their efforts to keep everyone informed the council issued regular press releases, posted notices around the market area and set up a webcam for those inclined to view the work in progress. It was perhaps the arrival of a giant tower crane on site which finally led doubters to believe that progress was in fact being made and that a new market hall would indeed emerge from the ashes. The mechanical monster which was to become a feature of the town centre skyline soon began hoisting huge concrete blocks and girders high into the sky perhaps emphasising that work now really was being done. A new basement was excavated which created storage room and space to accommodate the technical plant equipment for the building's air circulation. The tower crane which enabled materials to be loaded and unloaded to any part of the site was mounted upon a reinforced concrete base. This in turn was supported by piled foundations created especially for the purpose. New reinforced concrete pillars were installed to support the new basement which also provided a buttress for the building's remaining 'original' walls and the structure above.

It really was amazing just how much love the people of Ashton and indeed Tameside had for the old Market Hall. Over the years it held a special place in the hearts of traders and public alike, none more so than for Christina Kelly, who until her death on November 17th 2006 had an affection for the market quite unlike most people. This had started as a teenager when Christina, known to family and friends as Ena, resided in Marlborough Street, Ashton. However, it was not until 1984 after living in Scunthorpe for twenty-seven years did this affection really become so unique. Ena who had lost her husband in 1970 returned to Ashton rather than move to Birmingham with her daughter and son-in-law David. Ena decided to move back to be near to her sister and her beloved Ashton Market. She was adamant that her new home should be within easy walking distance of the market which was achieved with the purchase of a property on Beauchamp Street. From the very first day of her return daily visits to both market ground

Ena Kelly

and market hall became the norm, enjoying as she did the community spirit she found there. Ena struck up a close friendship with many of the traders and was on first name terms with most. Almost everything she ever bought was from the market or near by. Floor coverings, lamps, a three piece suite and other pieces of furniture came from there – traders would even give her a lift home in their vans. Ena bought most of her clothes including wedding outfits from the market as well as everyday items and food. *"She would bring muffins and meat pies galore on visits to us",* recalled daughter Rita. In her later years, although suffering failing eyesight it never stopped her daily trips to the market, as she could rely on the traders to help with her shop and to look after her, which they always did. After the devastating fire in 2004 Ena, like a great many people was bereaved at the loss of the market and the effect it had on her stall holder friends. With the opening of the Phoenix Market she remained steadfastly loyal to the traders who had moved there. In her 91st year no longer fit enough to make the journey Ena reluctantly had to accept the help of a weekly shopper. She would issue the shopper with her list and instructions as to which stalls to visit – and if the shopper got it wrong Ena was far from impressed. Sadly in November 2006 at the age of 93 years Ena died. As building work on the new market hall was in progress Rita contacted Tameside Council regarding the possibility of having her mother's ashes buried in the foundations. As indicated by Rita it seemed only fitting that the market hall should become her final resting place. The Council were touched by the huge affection Ena had for the market and although it was not normal practice they were happy to grant Rita's wishes. It was simply a case of waiting for the project to reach a suitable stage. This was to be in February 2008 at a special ceremony arranged and conducted by Revd David Hunter, Rita's husband. Consequently on Friday 22nd February Ena was once again reunited with her beloved market.

Rita Hunter (right) with husband Reverend David Hunter (centre) prior to interment of Ena Kelly

In July of 2008 twenty-eight schoolchildren were invited to see how the building was progressing. In a ceremony attended by Councillor Kieran Quinn the children placed in to a lead box a copy of the Tameside Advertiser's front page reporting on the fire, a DVD of shoppers' memories, a typical shopping list and coins of the realm. The box was then welded shut by Katrina Cain a plumbing student who had just passed her exams at Tameside College. The container was then encased in the brickwork of one of the cavity walls where a special plaque was placed stating that it would be reopened in 2058. The children selected from six local schools were each given a ticket inviting them back in fifty years time to the reopening of the capsule.

The summer of 2008 had proved to be a washout with above average amounts of rain which unavoidably also delayed building work by about one month. By August the crane which had loomed high above the market had been removed from the site and the new glass roof was almost complete. Shortly after, Tameside council gave the news which the whole town had been long awaiting. The £16.2million refurbishment was now nearing completion and an official opening date of Friday 28th November was announced. The countdown was now well and truly underway and as a lead-up to the big day the Market Hall's newly restored clock was unveiled on Friday 17th October. After the fire all that remained of the historic clock were three of its four frames, which protected the clock faces. These were repaired, but an identical replica had to be found to complete the four. As crowds gathered Councillor Quinn declared that the return of the clock to the town was an important landmark on the way to the reopening of the hall. He went on to say how the council had kept their guarantee that they would safeguard the heritage and history – *"The bits you don't see are much more modern and up to date but the face – a classic Westminster face – is the same. We never felt tempted to change it because it's too much a part of the iconic nature of the hall".* After the clock had chimed for the first time since May 2004 Tameside MBC executive leader Councillor Roy Oldham invited the crowds to follow the civic dignitaries to the top of the Market Avenue where the first of a series of bronze figures was unveiled. Councillor Oldham said, *"We are at a point where there is much to celebrate about Ashton's past and future".* The six sculptures unveiled included four children; a miner and a busker's open case and these pieces of impressive street furniture are all within easy walking distance of the market.

Councillor Roy Oldham unveils one of the six new sculptures

With the reopening day of the market hall fast approaching workers were still putting the finishing touches to the historic building. Gradually traders began to wind down business in the Phoenix Market and were transferring stock over to their new stalls. There were some which had ceased trading several weeks earlier in order to better prepare themselves. The layout of the new building was reminiscent to that of the old market with each stall being located as near as possible to their original position. The idea of having the stalls in a more regimented style similar to a supermarket layout had thankfully been resisted. Although most stalls were slightly smaller than their original counterparts few traders had any complaints, most were just glad to be eventually moving back 'home', especially in time for Christmas. Those trading on the outdoor market were just as eagerly awaiting their return as too were other shops and businesses as of course the loss of the market hall had affected them all.

Prior to the reopening 'The Tameside Advertiser' newspaper ran a series of articles which looked back at the market's history as well as reporting on latest developments. Similar articles were also run in the 'Tameside Reporter' all of which helped build up the anticipation of the people. With just weeks to go before the big event Tameside MBC in conjunction with both the local papers and Tameside Radio organised a competition the winner of which would officially open the restored market hall. Readers and listeners were invited to write in with their most lasting memory of their past visits to the market hall. Advertiser reader Carolyn Harrop was judged to be the winner with her childhood memory of sitting on the counter of a drinks stall with a milkshake for a treat while her mum drank hot Horlicks. As well as being chosen to take part in the official opening ceremony Carolyn also picked up £100 worth of vouchers to spend in the hall. Ada Brown from Ashton whom we had the pleasure of talking with while writing this additional chapter came second in the competition. Her memories of the Mark's & Spencer Penny Bazaar won her £50 in vouchers. Dukinfield resident Fred Hillson won vouchers worth £25 for his memory of the glistening mounds of tripe on display in the market.

Eventually the big day was upon us – the morning of November 28th 2008 saw many outdoor market traders arriving earlier than usual. Jason Beeley of the picture and frames stall on the market ground informed us that most traders had arrived at around 5.30am. It was a bitterly cold morning and early signs indicated not too many people were gathering to witness the event. Unlike the reopening of the outdoor market after the alterations of 1993 this event was to be a more low-key affair. This time around no expensive celebrity had been hired to conduct the ceremony, although in his field Barry McQueen who led proceedings is undoubtedly a celebrity. Barry, born Glyn Parry in Millbrook, Stalybridge is a seasoned campaigner having entertained audiences nationwide for years with his cabaret act. Now living in Blackpool he has the distinction of being elected the holiday resort's first official town crier, a role he carries out alongside those for

Tameside, Boddingtons and Virgin Trains. Barry is also a member of the Britannic Guild of Toastmasters and officiates at countless weddings all over the country. In his own inimitable style he hosted the well staged market hall reopening, which was a credit to the organisers and those taking part. Considering the timing of the event when the majority of shoppers had not yet ventured into town a fair sized crowd eventually gathered. Music from The Tame Valley Brass Ensemble filled the chilly air and their mixture of popular tunes and Christmas carols provided another reason other than the cold for onlookers to tap their feet. By the time the Barry McQueen officially opened proceedings with the 'The Post Horn Gallop' hundreds of shoppers surrounded the stage that had been set up in the Civic Square at the front of the Market Hall. The Mayor and Mayoresss of Tameside, Councillor Jack Davis and wife Carole, along with Councillor Kieran Quinn and Tameside Council Leader Roy Oldham were introduced to the crowds but the biggest cheer was reserved for competition winner Carolyn Harrop. A break in proceedings gave an opportunity for 'Mango Rose' a female aerial acrobatic act to thrill the onlookers. The warm response received must surely have thawed out the duo's bodies which were clad in not very appropriate costumes for the weather conditions. Following a rendition of 'Blue Moon' by the Brass Ensemble - which brought some humorous banter between footballing 'blue' Roy Oldham and 'red' Kieran Quinn - the main event got underway. Carolyn Harrop together with Councillor Quinn cut the ribbon as the '1812 Overture' boomed loud and the crowds were showered by a cascade of coloured paper fired with a bang from two confetti cannons. For the first time in over four years shoppers were once again entering into the market hall.

Tameside Honorary 'Town Crier' Millbrook born Glyn Parry today known as Barry McQueen

Crowds awaiting the reopening of the market

Rather than join the rush towards the market entrances we stepped aside for a while taking in the scene, after four years another few minutes wouldn't matter. While taking a few photographs we struck up a conversation with Ken Bebbington and his partner Joan, who to our surprise had travelled from the Falkland Islands to attend the market reopening.

Stall

S Williams & Sons
Outerwear

Ashton born Ken lives most of the year at a Falkland's military base where he works as an electrician. It was while on a visit home in 2004 that the tragic blaze occurred and he vowed he would be present the moment it rose from the ashes. *"I didn't think the council would rebuild it. I thought it would be knocked down, they have done a great job",* said Ken. Having grown-up in Ashton Ken had known the market since being a child and recalled how as a youngster he had once bought a brass curtain ring so he could 'marry' his mother. The day's proceedings had brought a tear to his eye and he remarked, *"The market is special and as one of the speakers had said it was like having its heart ripped out but now it's back again beating away. Today has been fantastic and well worth the journey".* Having finally entered the new market hall we seemed to be faced with a constant tidal wave of smiles, not once did we see a frown, ah yes once from a little girl whose mother had said no to sweets from Gleave's. As we walked slowly along each crowded aisle we passed many stalls with long queues – several traders must have anticipated this judging by the numbers of staff they had in attendance. What a different picture to that portrayed not so long ago at the Phoenix Market. Being back 'home' and with Christmas looming the traders were looking forward to good business.

Ken Bebbington and partner Joan travelled from the Falkland Islands for the Market reopening

In order to promote Ashton's newly reopened market hall to a wider public a TV advert was commissioned. The advertisement aired within 'Granadaland's' North West area and hit screens at a peak viewing time prior to 'Coronation Street'. Featuring one time 'Corrie' star Amanda Barrie it showed off the wonderful facilities of the new hall and with Amanda being an Ashton born lass everyone had great hopes the advert would get noticed.

Ashton born Amanda Barrie promoting the Market in a TV advert screened throughout North West

This was probably a foregone conclusion being screened as it was to an audience of millions. However, for many people, as the Internet later revealed, it was also noticed for other reasons. While the advert certainly got the message across by depicting Amanda enjoying the services of the market hall, she clearly wasn't there. Her acting was studio shot in front of a blue screen, a process known as chromakey, which simply means she was superimposed. There could have been many reasons why it had to be made this way, but the remark she made at the close of the advert about being an 'Ashton girl' and not actually being at the market brought about many comments. What does it matter you may think and to a point we agree.

The Ashton Civic Society is a body of people whose aims are to promote an awareness of the town's inheritance. They strive to preserve local buildings of an architectural and historical interest whilst promoting a high standard of structural design and planning. Annually the Society presents an award for the 'Building of the Year' – past recipients have included 'The Oddfellows Hall, Stamford Street, the New Charter Offices, Cavendish Street and 225 Old Street which houses the Pennine Care NHS Foundation Trust. It is quite fitting and a just reward for all the hard work involved that the winner of the Society's Award for 2008 should be the Market Hall. As commented upon by the Society's chairman Susan Knight, designs to meet the 21st Century have been incorporated into the listed building. Presenting the award to Councillor Quinn she said *"We are all delighted that the refurbished hall with its original outer walls and many features is now functioning once again – the heart has been put back into the town".*

The reopening of the market hall also saw the return of another refurbished grade II listed building. This was the red telephone box adjacent to the market hall on Bow Street. To avoid any damage occurring during the subsequent clean up after the fire and throughout the rebuilding programme the kiosk was fully encased within a protective wooden box. The General Post Office had introduced the first public phone box, kiosk1 (K1 Mk234) in 1921. It was made from reinforced concrete, with wooden door and window frames. The roof featured an ironwork spear and scrolls. A later modification (K1 Mk235) saw the wooden windows frames being replaced by ones of metal. It was a K1 box which first occupied the corner Bow Street/Market Street position until the mid-1930s (see photo on page 49).

Two Grade II Listed Buildings

The iconic red telephone box came about as a result of a competition held in 1924 to design a grander kiosk. Several noted architects submitted designs, including Sir Giles Gilbert Scott who went on to be the eventual winner. Scott was famous not only for his telephone boxes but also for his achievements in overseeing the post-WWII rebuilding work on the Houses of Parliament and the design of Liverpool Cathedral. The decision to paint the boxes red was taken so as to enable them to be easily seen in an emergency. Scott's design was designated as Kiosk 2 (K2) which was followed successively by K3, 4 and 5. For various reasons none of these were introduced nationwide on a large scale. Indeed this did not happen until 1936 when, from another design by Sir Giles Scott to commemorate the Silver Jubilee of King George V (1935), the first standard phone box to be used throughout the country was introduced. Thousands were deployed in virtually every town and city and the red telephone boxes, just like the red letter box and London buses, soon became a British icon. It was one of these K6 boxes which replaced the existing K1 box near to the market hall. Others also began to appear around town. The red phone box which was situated inside the market hall which was destroyed by the fire of 2004 was also a K6 but was not a listed building. A notable difference with this box to the one on Bow Street was that it carried the St Edward's Crown introduced by Queen Elizabeth after her coronation. Prior to 1952 all the boxes carried the Tudor Crown. The K6 boxes which were made of cast iron and weighed around three-quarters of a ton began to be replaced from the late 1980s by more modern ones. With the newly privatised BT announcing sweeping changes the end result saw many K6 boxes being removed from British streets. However, around 2000 red boxes were declared listed buildings and remain in place today. The Bow Street kiosk was listed as a Grade II building in 1987 and still stands proudly on its original site.

The remains of the phone box inside the market hall after the fire of 2004

On Monday 26th January 2009 the public, for the very first time, were able to see something which hitherto generations of Ashtonians had only ever heard. For on this day councillor Whitehead conducted a special ceremony within the market hall which saw the unveiling of the clock tower's historic bell. The bell which for years had faithfully announced the hours fell from its cross beam during the blaze of 2004. Although restoration work was carried out the bell still bears signs of the damage it sustained. A few weeks after the ceremony, a commemorative plaque was affixed to the nearby wall which gave a brief history of the market hall since its official opening on the site in 1830. Hopefully the area where the bell stands will eventually display other items and photographs relating the market's historic past.

Cllr Alan Whitehead paid tribute to the magnificent restoration of the market while unveiling the bell.

But what of the future? It was now widely accepted that the country was in a recession, trading on the 'High Street' was plummeting to a record low. Many major stores were facing closure with the most notable to cease trading being 'Woolworths'. The store had for many years operated an outlet in Ashton, firstly on Stamford Street, then Warrington Street before moving into the Arcades. Would the market be affected by the recession or would the public turn to it for their bargains?

No one knows what the future has in store but it is hoped that the market will continue to provide customers with what they want and traders with a living for many years to come. Ashton's market traders have always been at the forefront in reacting to customer needs by selling commodities in demand. On November 28th 2008 Ashton Market took its first breath in its new lease of life. Hopefully, it will stand firm against any future trends and remain a focal point within the community proving to everyone that come what may there will always be an Ashton Market.

‘*Wired to the Moon*’

Frank Randle – A Life

Frank Randle – was one of the great music hall comedians and arguably Britain’s greatest ever comic character actor. Today fifty years after his death the mention of his name still brings a smile to many faces. He was the major attraction for years in Blackpool summer shows and a star of low budget films, all box office successes. His own touring company ‘Randle’s Scandals’ packed theatres for over ten years. With his popularity however, came notoriety his name appearing in newspaper headlines almost as often as on theatre bills and his appearances in court were almost as frequent as those on stage. Drunken, violent, crazy, foul-mouthed and cunning are words which could describe Randle. But so too are gentle, kind, warm-hearted, generous and well-mannered. The authors’ through years of painstaking research have presented a ground-breaking account of a man who made an invaluable contribution to British comedy. They have tried to separate fact from fiction. Randle fans along with film buffs have bemoaned the lack of accessible material until now. This book may or may not alter your opinion of Randle, what it will do is give a fascinating look at his life.

“The life, and what a life, of this wild man of British comedy... is told in impressive detail in [Wired to the Moon]. A warts and all story of a man who, to this day, is regarded as possibly England’s finest comic actor. “Wired to the Moon is a fitting tribute to mark the 50th anniversary of [Randle’s] death. “Anyone who remembers Frank Randle with fondness will enjoy the book... ”. Oldham Evening Chronicle.

“The authors, through years of painstaking research, have presented a landmark account of a man who made an invaluable contribution to British comedy”.
Blackpool Gazette.

Order NOW from your bookshop at £15.99
or contact address on page iv for discounted price.

Published by History on your Doorstep
(HOYD Publications)
ISBN 0 9518012 5 2

Hooray for Jollywood

The Life of John E. Blakeley & The Mancunian Film Corporation

Originally published in 2001 this republication has been eagerly awaited by many. With slightly expanded text and amendments plus the inclusion of many more photos and illustrations this book is a must for any British cinema history buff.

John E. Blakeley was a rare breed in the annals of British film history for all the films he made were produced solely for northern audiences. Indeed, it's probably fair to say that they were despised in the south of the country. Through necessity, his films were initially shot in London, although they were planned and conceived in his home city of Manchester. Made on a shoestring budget and usually bereft of a storyline his stock company of popular northern music hall eccentrics made them extremely popular with the Lancashire working-classes. His stars included George Formby, Nat Jackley, Norman Evans, Duggie Wakefield, Jewel & Warriss, Josef Locke and of course the inimitable Frank Randle. In 1947 at a time when the film industry was virtually on its knees, Blakeley did the unthinkable and opened his own studio in Manchester. At a cost of £70,000, Film Studios (Manchester) was equipped and housed in an old Wesleyan Church, on Dickenson Road, Rusholme. Known locally as the 'Fun Factory' or 'Jollywood' the studio carried on turning out the popular comedies. This book tells the story of John E. Blakeley his lifetime in the film industry and of a devoted family man. It also looks behind the scenes of film making both in London and Manchester. Many stories are told of the stars that worked at 'Jollywood' and many are featured in this book.

"The book is a splendid evocation of a golden era of Mancunian and Lancastrian humour...a book I could happily read over and over again". **Manchester Evening News.**

"...a must for all movie buffs". **Tameside Reporter.**

"This book is a 'must-have' for anybody interested in the subject matter contained here. I cannot think of any other work which so comprehensively tells us about this much-missed man and the films he made".
Peter Pollard - George Formby Society

Order NOW from your local bookshop priced £15.99
or contact address on page iv for discounted price.
Published by History on your Doorstep
ISBN 978 0 9518012 9 1

ALSO AVAILABLE BY POST ONLY

'FRANK RANDLE'S FILM FUN'

The Comic Strip antics of film comedian Frank Randle Culled from the pages of Vintage 'Film Fun' Annuals and Comics.

Randle first appeared in the British Comic 'Film Fun' in 1947 and continued until 1955 two years after he had made his last film' and two years before he died. Now many of the comedian's 'Film Fun' cartoon strips have been brought together for the first time in this publication.

'Randle's Film Fun' is sure to become a collectors' item - Make sure of your copy now - Not available in the shops - Only Available by post from HOYD Publications. Telephone: 0161 308 3013 for payment details.

Over 100 pages of vintage laughter
Priced at £9.99 plus £1.30 p&p.